W9-CPG-568

CONSUMING THE CONGO

WAR AND CONFLICT MINERALS
IN THE WORLD'S DEADLIEST PLACE

PETER EICHSTAEDT

Lawrence Hill Books

Library of Congress Cataloging-in-Publication Data
Eichstaedt, Peter H., 1947–
  Consuming the Congo : war and conflict minerals in the world's deadliest
place / Peter Eichstaedt.
     p. cm.
  Includes bibliographical references and index.
  ISBN-13: 978-1-56976-310-0
  ISBN-10: 1-56976-310-0
  1. Congo (Democratic Republic)—History—1997– 2. Massacres—Congo
(Democratic Republic) 3. Massacres—Congo (Democratic Republic)—Ituri.
4. Mines and mineral resources—Congo (Democratic Republic) 5. Genocide—
Congo (Democratic Republic) 6. Rape victims—Congo (Democratic Republic)
7. Children—Violence against—Congo (Democratic Republic) 8. International
Criminal Court. 9. Congo (Democratic Republic)—Ethnic relations. 10. Ituri
(Congo)—Ethnic relations. I. Title.
  DT658.26.E34 2011
  967.5103'4—dc22

                                                                2011004944

Interior design: Jonathan Hahn
Map design: Chris Erichsen
Photos: © Peter Eichstaedt

Published by Lawrence Hill Books
An imprint of Chicago Review Press, Incorporated
814 North Franklin Street
Chicago, Illinois 60610
ISBN: 978-1-56976-310-0
Printed in the United States of America
5 4 3 2 1

"The conflict in the Democratic Republic of the Congo has become mainly about access, control and trade of five key mineral resources: coltan, diamonds, copper, cobalt and gold. The wealth of the country is appealing and hard to resist in the context of lawlessness and the weakness of the central authority."

> —United Nations Security Council, *Report of the Panel of Experts on the Illegal Exploitation of Natural Resources and Other Forms of Wealth of the Democratic Republic of the Congo*

"The white man is very clever. He came quietly and peaceably with his religion. We were amused at his foolishness and allowed him to stay. Now he has won our brothers, and our clan can no longer act like one. He has put a knife on the things that held us together and we have fallen apart."

> —Chinua Achebe, *Things Fall Apart*

CONTENTS

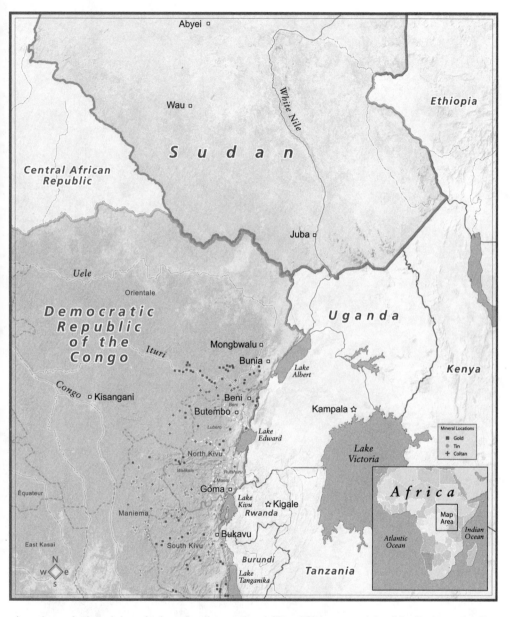

Locations of mineral deposits based on International Alert, "Gisements miniers" in *Etude sur le rôle de l'exploitation des ressources naturelles dans l'alimentation et la perpétuation des crises de l'est de la RDC* (London: International Alert, October 2009), 90. For more information, see *Crossed Crocodiles*, "Trading Congo Contraband," February 21, 2010, http://crossedcrocodiles.wordpress.com/2010/02/21 /trading-congo-contraband-maps-3t-minerals-coltan-gold/.

PROLOGUE

THE GATES OF HELL

KING LEOPOLD of Belgium claimed the country now known as the Democratic Republic of the Congo as his personal property in the 1870s, setting in motion one of the most monstrous plunders ever by a colonial power. Ivory, gold, rubber, and an array of minerals were taken in his name, along with millions of lives. But the plunder did not end with the Congo's independence in the mid-1960s—it intensified under the corrupt thirty-two-year regime of Mobutu Sese Seko that ended in 1997. In the years since, the pillage and bloodletting in the Congo have continued at a frightening pace. Some five million Congolese died unnecessarily from 1998 to 2007, according to the International Rescue Committee, making it the worst toll on human life since World War II. Yet the carnage has gone largely unnoticed in the outside world.

These killing fields are concentrated in the Congo's eastern provinces of North and South Kivu and northward into the Ituri region of the sprawling Province Orientale. It is a no-man's-land where the Congo, Rwanda, Uganda, Burundi, and Tanzania meet. This remote and lawless region happens to be one of the world's richest sources of gold, diamonds, timber, and, more recently, minerals such as tin and coltan, both critical to the high-tech circuitry found in cell phones, computers, and other popular electronics.

Marauding militias and renegade army units control these mines, lording over miners who dig with picks, shovels, and iron bars. Their profits allow these armed men to roam the jungle forests, killing and raping at will. Most militias descend from remnants of the armies who carried out the 1994 Rwandan genocide. Rwanda's Tutsi government and army drove their ethnic rival Hutu *génocidaires* out of Rwanda and into eastern Congo, creating a cauldron of chaos far beyond the control of the Congo's distant capital, Kinshasa.

A state of war has burned throughout the region since 1996 and seems to be the sole news story emerging from eastern Congo. The conflict masks the extensive and frequently illicit exploitation of mineral wealth in the region. Local populations are left with lives of grueling manual labor and exposure to brutality, death, and disease. This exploitation and deprivation continue under the watchful eyes of a UN force of twenty-thousand-plus soldiers tasked with keeping a peace that does not exist. Despite the persistent mayhem, the United Nations is beginning a drawdown of forces in mid-2011 that will leave the beleaguered eastern Congolese to an unknown fate. Because of international concerns, however, the drawdown is riddled with contingencies, largely based on the progress toward peace in various regions.

My first taste of the chaos in eastern Congo came in the spring of 2006, when I paused in the shade of towering trees at the border between eastern Congo and Uganda, an expanse marked by a twisted and wobbly wire fence. The dirt road was filled with fleeing Congolese silently carrying whatever they could: a tin cooking pot, a plastic wash basin, a bedroll. One woman passed with a fifty-gallon steel drum balanced on her head, leading a couple of children dressed in rags. Most had only the clothes on their backs. The tread of their steps was the only sound.

I had come from a refugee camp nearby where several thousand Congolese had just spent the night. The camp was nothing more than a grassy field with a few portable toilets and a UN truck dispensing meager supplies and packets of high-energy cookies. Fear hung in the air like the fog that surrounded us and was impervious to the searing equatorial sun. As I talked with the refugees, I found that behind their fear was anger.

These Congolese were ethnic Hutus running from the renegade Tutsi general Laurent Nkunda, who had vowed to protect his ethnic brothers and sisters from the Hutu militias that once plagued the eastern Congo. These militias were incarnations of the notorious Hutu *interahamwe* who carried out the 1994 Rwandan genocide. The Rwandan nightmare had not really ended. It just moved across the border.

Although the flight of refugees was steady, there was no panic. It was hard to imagine that these refugees were the same people who had participated in the bloody deaths of nearly eight hundred thousand Tutsis in just three months, some twelve years earlier. At the camp, hollow-eyed children roamed barefoot, wearing dirty, threadbare clothes, while their parents sprawled on the ground, exhausted, using a rolled-up jacket or an arm for a pillow. Human feces littered the field. Refugees told me of trying to make a living, of trying to raise a family, of trying to live a normal life.

Forced to flee their homes, they now huddled under plastic tarps that provided little protection from the frigid mountain air that swept into the valley most nights. An estimated twenty thousand Congolese poured into Uganda that week, catching relief workers by surprise and leaving them to pass out plastic containers for water—although there was no immediate source of clean water available—along with cups and thin gray blankets given to men who clutched them closely and ducked into the crowd.

The Congolese said they'd "rather die here" than face death at home. When I asked why the Congolese Tutsis were attacking them, one said the Tutsis wanted to make their own state inside eastern Congo.

It was unlikely but not impossible. The Democratic Republic of the Congo is roughly the size of Europe. The seat of government is far to the west in Kinshasa, separated from the eastern provinces by a vast and roadless jungle that makes travel virtually impossible except by foot or air. Kinshasa has little control over the eastern provinces. Except for the UN peacekeepers in eastern Congo, there is little law and order. What does exist depends on which militia controls a region or village.

Eastern Congo is a patchwork generally controlled by any of four key groups. The most feared is the ethnic Hutu militia known as the Democratic Forces for the Liberation of Rwanda, known by the French acronym FDLR. Another is the former Tutsi militia, the National Congress for the Defense of the People, known by another French acronym, CNDP. The third is the Mai-Mai, composed largely of home-grown militias with a fondness for amulets, witchcraft, and spirits. The final group is the increasingly powerful Congolese national army, whose strength grows as it incorporates these militias into its ranks.

As I stood on the border of the Congo that day, I wondered how a decade of death and destruction—six times worse than the Rwandan genocide—could have taken place in eastern Congo, just across the border from Rwanda, while the world still bemoaned the horror that had happened in Rwanda. Despite the hand-wringing and sighing over Rwanda, few paid attention to eastern Congo.

I crossed the border into the Congo that day in 2006 and nervously walked the dirt streets of the little border town known as Bunagana. Shops were boarded. People huddled quietly in a makeshift market, stealing glances as I passed, displaying cabbages, potatoes, and a few slabs of fly-covered goat meat. Around a corner, I encountered heavily armed soldiers wearing variously colored berets, fatigue pants, and T-shirts—some toting high-caliber machine guns and RPGs. They fingered their weapons and glared.

I returned to eastern Congo in 2008 and again in 2009, driven to unearth what was behind the bloodshed that plagued the region. I traveled the countryside to hear the stories of those who lived this nightmarish reality. There was the woman who served up homemade brew in Bunia; the women raped by militia fighters; villagers who uncovered piles of human bones; former child soldiers who dug for gold in knee-deep muck; miners who chipped away at chunks of rock for coltan; refugees who were chased from their mountain villages as renegade militias fought over mines; and the suave mineral dealers of Goma.

Eastern Congo defies comparison. The loss of life far exceeds deaths in Iraq and Afghanistan combined. Yet this is not some distant tragedy, not just another African horror story. The lives and deaths of these millions of Congolese are linked to us all. The mines that scar the verdant hills and mountains of eastern Congo produce a very small but very bloody portion of the tin and coltan metal that is critical to our modern lives. Each time we use a mobile phone, use a video game console, or open a tin can, we hold the lives and deaths of the eastern Congolese in our hands.

1

THE *MANDRO* HUT

THE AIR is thick and beery in this crowded mud-and-thatch hut.
The woman brewing the mealy beer they call *mandro* wears
a bright wrap and fills a gourd for me, insisting that I drink. When
I refuse the frothy mix, something like runny oatmeal, she bellows
a drunken curse about this rude foreigner to the amusement of her
customers.

I'm in Bunia, the heart of the Ituri region in northeastern Democratic Republic of the Congo. Dusty streets and pockmarked buildings
lend Bunia the look of a Wild West movie set. Far from a Hollywood
fantasy, this town is deadly real. At one of the main intersections, a
pyre of sandbags is topped by a machine gun manned by two soldiers
wearing the blue helmets of the UN peacekeepers. These soldiers have
a commanding view and guard the entrance to the UN's compound,
an outpost of civilization in this lawless and blood-soaked part of
the world. With me is Jacques Kahorha, a Congolese journalist from
Goma, the capital of the North Kivu province.

A mild euphoria has been wafting through town. It is late June
2008, and one of the town's favorite sons, former militia leader Thomas
Lubanga, is about to go on trial at the International Criminal Court
(ICC) in The Hague, Netherlands. He's been charged with conscripting child soldiers from among his ethnic Hema community to fight

against the more populous ethnic Lendu. The trial has drawn world-wide attention as the first international case to highlight the problem of child soldiers. It is also the ICC's first case to go to trial, despite its nearly six years of existence as the world's first permanent war crimes court. But just as expectations peak, the court suspends the trial in a dispute over evidence. Ironically, the suspension won't be the only one to plague the trial, which will eventually stretch on for years. This initial suspension, however, has many in Bunia convinced that Lubanga is on his way home after more than two years in jail in The Hague waiting for his trial to start.

Bunia is at the heart of what has plagued eastern Congo, by far the deadliest region in the world, outstripping Iraq, Colombia, and Afghanistan combined. The most reliable information about this dubious honor comes from a study by the International Rescue Committee released in early 2008. Based on research conducted over the previous ten years, 5.4 million "excess deaths" occurred across the Congo from August 1998 to April 2007, deaths above and beyond what normally would have occurred without war. An estimated 2 million deaths came after a peace deal was signed in the country in 2002. More than 3 million were killed in the Congo's mineral-rich eastern provinces.

Five million dead in a span of ten years makes this—called Africa's First World War—the deadliest human catastrophe since World War II, but, save for occasional articles in the back pages of major newspapers and magazines, and sporadic books, hardly anyone outside Africa knows about it. Though most people have heard of the genocide in neighboring Rwanda, which pales in comparison, I marvel at how a tragedy of this magnitude could have been so thoroughly ignored. This tsunami of mortality has not been random killing at the hands of a few renegades. It has been the result of a vicious civil war that started in 1996, then erupted again in 1998, and involved at least five other African countries. It has flared continuously ever since.

I am in eastern Congo not to cover a war but for something quite different. As Africa Editor for the Institute for War & Peace Reporting at the time and based in The Hague, I'm here to lead a workshop for journalists who report on the ICC's efforts to bring those responsible for the killing to trial. At that moment, the ICC holds three men from the region in custody and is preparing a trial for a fourth, Jean-Pierre Bemba, the Congo's former vice president and 2006 presidential candidate. Bemba lost a runoff election to the current president, Joseph Kabila. Just weeks before I arrived in Bunia, Bemba was arrested in Belgium, and he awaits extradition to The Hague. Bemba's first hearing at the ICC will take place in early January 2009, and his trial will be subsequently and repeatedly rescheduled. Bemba's trial will finally begin on November 22, 2010.

Underlying the internecine violence in eastern Congo has been a dizzying array of militias spawned by ancient ethnic animosities. In the Ituri region, it is the Lendu and Hema tribes, the two largest ethnic groups in the region. The Lendu and Hema are just two of the more than two hundred ethnicities scattered across the Congo and speaking a wide array of languages and dialects.

In this thatch-and-mud beer hut on the Hema side of town, my questions, as well as the brew, unleash years of pent-up anger against their ethnic Lendu rivals.

"We want to know the crime that [Lubanga] committed," the proprietor hollers, waving her empty serving gourd. "They came to rescue us," she says of Lubanga's swarm of boy soldiers. "We were running with kids in our arms. He came to help us." She points at the dirt road outside the hut. "Five were killed right there."

"People were trying to kill us," says another woman, cradling a gourd of the foamy brew. "They were Lendu. He [Lubanga] helped us so much. They're telling lies," she says of the ICC. The militia was composed of child soldiers, she says, but it was a matter of necessity, not criminality. "Maybe they came and killed your family," she says of the child soldiers, some of whom were orphaned and had to choose between picking up a gun or starving to death. "It's better to be a soldier. Children were joining as a way to protect themselves." She points to one of the customers. "He's an orphan. The Lendu killed everyone in his village."

Resentment against the international court is palpable. As people speak, I ask for their names, but they refuse, telling me that if they are identified in print or on the Internet, ICC investigators will drag them to the court in The Hague and force them to testify against Lubanga. They'd rather die.

"When someone comes to kill you, what do you do?" asks a man sitting beside me. "You defend yourself. That's what [Lubanga] did." Because of this, he claims, Lubanga should not be on trial.

But Lubanga's arrest has not been a mistake. Lubanga's full name is Thomas Lubanga Dyilo, and he was apprehended on March 17, 2006, for his activities as leader of the notorious Union of Congolese Patriots (UPC). After he sat in the ICC jail for ten months, the court finally confirmed the charges against him, meaning that the judges were satisfied that the evidence against Lubanga was enough to put him on trial. He stands charged with war crimes, specifically conscripting and enlisting children under the age of fifteen into the UPC and using them to fight throughout the Ituri region from September 2002 to August 2003.

Also in ICC custody at the time are two other militia leaders from Ituri who fought against Lubanga: Germain Katanga and Mathieu Ngudjolo, both of whom are ethnic Lendu. A third militia leader from the region, Bosco Ntaganda, fought with Lubanga's group and is also indicted by the ICC. After fighting in the Ituri region as Lubanga's top commander, Ntaganda became the deputy commander for another militia leader, General Laurent Nkunda, whose ethnic Tutsi militia controls the mineral-laden hills of the Masisi in North Kivu, far to the south of Ituri. Ntaganda subsequently joined the Congolese army and remains free.

The ICC has been focused on the Ituri region of the Congo for years, even before it issued indictments against Joseph Kony, the leader of Ugandan rebel group the Lord's Resistance Army, which fought a vicious and senseless war in northern Uganda for over twenty years.[1]

Because the ICC has interviewed hundreds of people in and around Bunia, many of whom witnessed or participated in the killings that swept the area, the beer drinkers are understandably wary. Since most foreigners they have met are affiliated with mining companies, the ICC, or the aid groups that prowl the region, these in the hut suspect me of spying for the ICC because that is what I keep asking them about.

My fear that the beer drinkers have little or no concept of the international court is quickly dispelled, however, when one *mandro* drinker complains about the court's postponement of Lubanga's trial and his rumored release. He pokes a finger into the air and shouts, "We don't understand why they have postponed [the case] so many times." Before I can offer an explanation, he provides his own answer: "It shows that the ICC cannot take control of the case." Keeping Lubanga in jail for two years without a trial is simply more colonial oppression, he says. "The whites are behind this."

The man's friend chimes in, saying that the Lubanga situation is rooted in ethnic-based political maneuvering, not fact. "It sounds like politics. They don't understand what happened. The ICC didn't get all the information."

"The ICC is unable to judge Thomas Lubanga," the first man adds. "He should be brought back here. For peace to resurface, he has to come back."

What confounds most in the *mandro* hut is that Lubanga has been charged with using child soldiers. This has been a common practice, however deplorable. More important, it pales in comparison with the horrific massacres that took place in the villages of their ethnic Hema kin and went far beyond the bounds of conventional warfare.

"The people who know what [Lubanga] did live here," a woman says, arguing that the judges in the Netherlands can never render a sound judgment because they will never know what happened in Ituri, or why.

"Thomas Lubanga worked for peace," says a young man.

"The voice of Ituri is not being heard," says another.

"The killers are not here. They're in power in Kinshasa," says yet another.

"Instead of arresting the killers, they arrested Thomas Lubanga," shouts still another.

Word has spread quickly that a foreigner is asking questions about Lubanga, and the beer hut has gotten crowded. Emotions run high as the proprietor serves gourd after gourd of *mandro*. The palpable tension becomes laced with anger, and I nod to Kahorha that it's time to leave. Kahorha nods back as he translates a torrent of comments. Kahorha has been in these situations before, having worked for some of the world's top news organizations, including CNN and the BBC. We edge toward the door as people shout over one another, Kahorha continuing to translate as I scribble notes. We push through bodies jammed at the entrance and dash for the car, leaving the drinkers behind. The car doors slam, and we barrel down the road, trailed by a plume of dust.

"We left not a moment too soon," I say with a big sigh.

Kahorha smiles. "Well, you wanted to talk to some folks . . ."

We are on our way to the Lendu side of town to get another take on the deadly fighting that has gripped Ituri. The drive gives me a moment to think. One of the *mandro* drinkers said the killers were in Kinshasa, the Congolese capital, so I ask Kahorha about that. Some of those who commanded militias in Ituri have become part of the Congolese government establishment or members of the Congolese military, Kahorha explains. Despite the crimes they may have committed in the eastern provinces of the Congo, they are now protected by their government status.

It has been part of a government policy, Kahorha continues, to defuse the war by enticing the militia leaders to abandon their commands in exchange for government or military posts. This removes them from the battlefield and draws them into the central government—the same entity they've fought so fiercely in the past. The hope, of course, is to bridge the gap between the Congo's disparate eastern and western provinces, a gap that is not only cultural and linguistic but also geographic.

The problem with this policy is precisely what angers the *mandro* drinkers: no justice. Those who may have been responsible for the most heinous of crimes are now living large in the national capital. But not all. Since the Congo is among the 111 nations who agree to support the ICC, it is obligated to arrest those indicted by the court. The Congo has complied by arresting Lubanga, Katanga, and Ngudjolo. But others are still free who the *mandro* drinkers know were involved in the region's violent history, and they can't understand why only certain people are arrested. To them, the court is political, not judicial.

BEFORE WE get to the Lendu side of town, Kahorha says we have to make a stop. Just off the main road in Bunia and within sight of the UN compound is a placid complex of whitewashed buildings that houses the offices of Caritas, the Catholic charity. Here I find Father Alfred Ndrabu, who heads the local Peace and Justice Commission under the auspices of the Bunia diocese. It is one of many such commissions set up throughout the Congo to collect information and monitor the progress of peace, or the lack thereof, in Ituri. The Bunia commission was established in October 2003 to accept the child soldiers released by Lubanga's militia and reintegrate them into society. "It was very difficult," Ndrabu says with a heavy sigh.

In the wake of the region's heaviest fighting, Ndrabu and the other Catholic priests began working toward community reconciliation by talking with key members of their congregations in and around Bunia, some of which included both Hema and Lendu. The goal was to get them just to talk to each other and hopefully defuse the ethnic tensions that had divided the town. It began to work. "People started talking to each other," he says, and neighbors began to trust each other. Then, in March 2006, Lubanga was arrested and turned over to the ICC, sending a shockwave through the community and causing the Hema and the Lendu to step back. "The confidence among people diminished a bit. Most of the people withdrew from each other. They couldn't understand how all the killing in the area could be the burden of just [Lubanga]."

The violence wasn't due only to Lubanga's militia, Ndrabu says. But he was the first one to be arrested, and the Hema community became suspicious because Lubanga had cooperated with authorities and released his child soldiers. More important, Ndrabu points out, Lubanga was not the only one responsible for the UPC as a political entity and a militia. "Those who pushed him to fight committed many crimes," he explains. The child soldiers who filled the militia were not necessarily forced. "The children joined him in order to survive."

Yet this desperate circumstance has been ignored by the ICC. "This is not adapted to reality," Ndrabu says of the ICC charges against Lubanga. "Recruitment of child soldiers was not new." The practice had emerged years earlier, when the late Laurent-Désiré Kabila, the former Congolese president, swept through the region in 1996 on his way to Kinshasa, where he toppled the government of Mobutu Sese Seko. Not only did Kabila's army use child soldiers, but so did the regional militias. "How can [the ICC] now only charge one person for what all have done?" he asks.

I have no answer. But the reasoning of the court, despite the apparent lopsidedness of the case, is that the international community must start someplace with the prosecution of those who use child soldiers. Lubanga was an obvious target and most likely will not be the last.

People in Ituri, Ndrabu explains, want to see those responsible for the mass killings in the region face justice, either in the Congo or abroad. "For local people, they want to see those who killed sixty thousand people in all the communities to be arrested." Ndrabu applauds the arrest of the Lendu militia leaders, Katanga and Ngudjolo, because it has defused some of the inter-ethnic tension. Regardless, people in Bunia have a hard time understanding why the slaughter of an entire village is not considered a crime worse than the recruitment of child soldiers.

"The community does not understand." If the ICC wants respect, it has to explain that, Ndrabu says. "Most people don't know the procedures." Many in the community think Lubanga is already dead. "It's better if [Lubanga] appears" in person at some point so that the Hema know their hero is still alive. It would help dispel misconceptions.

Most people "think he is a political prisoner." The people of Ituri distrust the ICC. "When they arrest those in government and with the power, then people will begin to trust the ICC."

WE CONTINUE through Bunia, past the UN compound, and make our way down dirt roads deep into a jumble of block homes and mud-and-thatch huts. This is the Lendu side of town. We park and walk under towering trees and beside neatly hoed gardens of corn, beans, and vegetables. We settle into low chairs on the hard-packed dirt that fronts a few mud-brick homes while we wait for Ernest Peke, a Lendu community leader. It's a long wait, and as the day fades, we watch women and children finish eating dinner. A chicken aggressively pecks food from a child's hand until he swats it away. African music floats over the women's murmuring voices, punctuated by an occasional child's cry. Just as darkness descends, Peke appears.

He's a lean man in his midfifties, possessing a leathery face creased by time. He wears a brown sport coat over a pressed shirt, trousers, and sandals. He has seen the best of times and the worst of times, he tells me, mimicking the opening line of Charles Dickens's novel *A Tale of Two Cities*.

He gestures to the house behind me. "There was a big house here," he says. "It was all destroyed." To understand Ituri, I need to go a short distance back in time, he tells me.

Hovering over everything like a curse are the highly prized minerals in the Ituri region. "There are so many resources here that are held by the communities," he states. Before the mid-1990s, life between the Hema and the Lendu was not so bad. "Conflicts existed, but fights would only last one day. They would compromise and make a deal."

The Ituri region's descent into chaos began in early 1996 with the arrival of the late Laurent Kabila's army, Peke says. Bunia fell to him in November 1996 with the help of Rwandan and Ugandan forces. As Kabila marched toward Kinshasa, the late President Mobutu's hopelessly corrupted Congolese military collapsed. Mobutu fled the Congo and died on September 17, 1997, in exile in Morocco.

Mobutu provoked the Rwandan invasion when he openly supported the Rwandan Hutu extremists responsible for the Rwandan genocide, who had fled into the eastern provinces after the Tutsi army chased them out of Rwanda in late 1994. The Hutus then formed a strong militia, the FDLR. The tense situation in the region was exacerbated in November 1996 when Mobutu ordered all the region's ethnic Tutsi to leave the Congo or be killed. The order outraged many, especially the Tutsi who were native Congolese and who began forming their own militias. Mobutu's anti-Tutsi actions precipitated his demise.

While regime change brought hopes that the massive corruption that plagued the Congo might end, Kabila has proven not up to the task, Peke says.

Not long after assuming power, Kabila dismissed his Rwandan military staff and ministers in a move to assert his Congolese credentials and show the country that he was not simply the tool of neighboring Uganda and Rwanda, two countries that are but a fraction of the size of the Congo. However, Kabila's actions infuriated Uganda and Rwanda. In early 1998 the two countries launched a second drive on Kinshasa, intent on deposing the renegade Kabila.

Back in Bunia, Peke explains, those in the Ituri region were again ready to help the Ugandans and Rwandans overthrow Kabila, since they, too, were disenchanted with the new regime. He says, "At the beginning, all came here to fight [against] Kabila's troops." Called the Rally for Congolese Democracy (RCD), the new army included not only Rwandan and Ugandan troops but also a strong militia led by Jean-Pierre Bemba, the powerful northern Congolese leader and son of one of the country's wealthiest businessmen.

But the second drive toward Kinshasa stalled when the Rwandans and Ugandans encountered heavy opposition in the northern provincial capital of Kisingani, center of the Congolese diamond trade. To save his regime, Kabila appealed to neighboring Angola, Namibia, and

Zimbabwe. Each country eagerly jumped into the fray, expecting to help itself to some of the Congo's resources.

As the war bogged down, Uganda and Rwanda carved out their own territories in eastern Congo, helping themselves to the abundant minerals. As the second war became less and less winnable, the two countries parted ways, each forming proxy militias that helped them plunder the region's gold, diamonds, timber, and coltan deposits.

"It was a serious looting," Peke tells me in the flickering light of a kerosene lantern. These years were a miasma of militias and changing loyalties as Lendu, Hema, and the Congolese government jockeyed for power and control.

Despite a peace agreement in August 1999, in which the warring parties agreed to a cease-fire, the fighting continued, because the Ugandan and Rwandan troops refused to withdraw, Peke says. The Hema used lulls in the fighting to build militias. Uganda set up camps and took young recruits to Uganda for training. The ultimate purpose, Peke says, was so Uganda could "exploit the minerals freely because the Lendu presented an obstacle."

The first attacks on Bunia's Lendu communities came in January 2001, forcing the Lendu to organize, Peke says. The Lendu lost a lot of men but captured enough arms and ammunition to mount a counteroffensive, attacking the Ugandan military in its base at the Bunia airport. Initially, Uganda had worked with Lubanga and the UPC, but it switched sides when it found that Lubanga was also working with the Rwandans.

Uganda shifted support to the Lendu, Peke says, making it clear that Uganda was only using the Hema and Lendu to its advantage. With the two ethnic groups pitted against each other, the chaos provided good cover for plunder. "The purpose was to have these groups fighting so they could settle down and take the resources," he states.

Under international pressure, Uganda eventually withdrew from Ituri in April 2003, and the Lendu protected the Ugandans' departure. Resentful, the Hema attacked the Ugandans at the Bunia airport, prompting a swift response from the Lendu, who swept through Bunia and drove Lubanga and the UPC out.

But the fighting was far from over. In early May 2003, Lubanga counterattacked and overran Bunia. At this point, the Congolese government finally stepped in and divided Bunia into two parts: one for Hema, another for Lendu. So it remains.

Lubanga is not at fault for what happened in Ituri, Peke tells me. "I met with him and he explained what happened. He was blocked by others. He now pays for the bad behavior of his community." Everyone knows about the recruitment of child soldiers. "Each [Hema] family was obliged to provide a son to his army. Each businessman had to contribute." And if he didn't, he could be killed. "I know [of] one in my village who was killed because he refused to contribute," he says. The Hema defended themselves against the attacks by Lendu leaders such as Germain Katanga. "Most of the killing happened at night. Many children lost their parents, so it was easy for them to join these [militia] groups [as child soldiers]. For others, [joining] was a curiosity."

Although a Lendu, Peke is disappointed with the delays in Lubanga's ICC trial. "The Hema are very disgusted," Peke states. "This is the same for the Lendu. They'd like to know what happened. This [trial] should be done as quickly as possible. If the ICC has no evidence, then [it] should release them." He is speaking of Lubanga, Katanga, and Ngudjolo. "Just keeping them in jail is not good for anybody." The militia leaders were arrested just as peace was taking hold in the community, he explains, disrupting an important trend. "Some were helping to turn in weapons, but they were arrested and put in jail."

Peke suddenly stops. It is pitch black and quiet, save the occasional chirp of a cricket and the low hiss of the kerosene lantern. Peke looks at me and smiles, his face blurred by the flickering flame, still perplexed and shaken by Bunia's decade of death. He sits quietly, hands on his knees, as if wondering why and how he survived. We have only scratched the surface. There is a Hema village not far from Bunia that was overrun repeatedly. That's where I go.

2

VILLAGE OF THE SKULLS

THE VILLAGE of Bogoro sits on a grassy knoll about fifteen miles southeast of Bunia. People raise crops and animals, sometimes selling them to buy the few amenities they can enjoy. The village strings along a road that rises to a crossroads, with one branch continuing eastward, winding into the distant hills and ending at Kisenyi, a fishing village on the shores of Lake Edward. The road gives the region access to people and goods boated from Uganda. Another road leads south, connecting to towns and communities in southern Ituri. Less than a day's walk from Bunia, Bogoro sits at a strategic location. Whoever controls Bogoro controls access to Bunia from the east and south.

Just below the surface of this pastoral setting simmer the memories of repeated massacres that decimated the village. One in particular took place on February 24, 2003, eventually compelling the attention of the International Criminal Court.

Again I am with Congolese journalist Jacques Kahorha, who has contacted a friend and colleague in Bunia, Richard Pituwa, an entrepreneur who owns one of the town's independent radio stations, Canal Revelation, or the Revelation Channel. One of Pituwa's pickup trucks sports the faded logo of a long-gone aid group. We accept his offer to take the truck since we're headed out of Bunia. The logo, he explains, looks just official enough that it might ease our passage through any random roadblocks thrown up by scheming locals to collect "safe passage" fees.

Our arrival in Bogoro stirs immediate attention. Samuel Bahemuka Mugeni, the village chief, invites us to sit with him in hastily arranged chairs in the packed dirt at the center of the village. Bogoro is predominately Hema, Mugeni explains, and that has meant the deaths of hundreds of villagers, entire families in some cases, and the loss of houses and animals—a family's primary measure of wealth. "This village was occupied by different militias," he says with a grimace.

The first of the massacres came in January 2001. "At the time, these Lendu came here to attack," Mugeni continues. Word of the impending attack was sent to the Ugandan army, which controlled the Bunia airport and which had sided with the Hema. The villagers prayed that Ugandan soldiers would arrive in time. The attacking militia was the Front for National Integration (FNI), formed by Lendu political leaders and regional chiefs to counter the rising strength and influence of the Hema's homegrown group, the Union of Congolese Patriots (UPC), led by Thomas Lubanga.

It was a bloody attack. "They came in the day, at 11:00 A.M., from the Blue Mountains." Mugeni gestures to the distant hills. "They didn't come to look, only to kill. They came with machetes, arrows, and hatchets. Those who were lucky escaped and went to Kisenyi."

The Ugandan army arrived late in the day, and by 9:00 P.M. had pushed the FNI units out of the village. Yet the village was far from safe. "The Lendu came the next day and attacked again," he says. When the day's slaughter ended, the village counted ninety-eight deaths. They began the gruesome task of burying the dead.

The attack provoked an immediate and violent response. In the nearby ethnic Hema villages, fighters mobilized and attacked the surrounding Lendu villages. "It's a matter of revenge," Mugeni explains. "They [the Lendu] knew [Bogoro] was a Hema village."

A year later, in February 2002, as the village of Bogoro was still recovering from its devastating losses, a meeting was called to end the vicious cycle of ethnic violence. A coalition had been formed by some of Ituri's key leaders, and among the participants was a group led by Jean-Pierre Bemba, the wealthy and influential leader from northern Congo. Bemba had been supported by Uganda. Also joining the coalition was Bemba's rival, Mbusa Nyamwisi, a local warlord know widely as Mbusa, and his militia, the Rally for Congolese Democracy (RCD), which had also been formed with the help of the Ugandans. Finally, there was Lubanga's Hema militia, the UPC.

The militias were to meet at the Bunia soccer stadium and bring their weapons, Mugeni explains. It was not for a final shootout but for the weapons to be ceremoniously burned and buried. The event happened, a feast was shared, and reconciliation was to commence. It was a nice idea.

As the celebrants of peace returned home the next day, they were ambushed. The attackers were the Lendu, Mugeni says, and the situation in Bunia quickly deteriorated. Mbusa's militia attacked the Hema communities, and this in turn brought reprisals from Lubanga's UPC militia.

Mugeni gazes with war-weary eyes as I put down my pen for a moment. He has the air of a battered and angry man who has suffered more than any one person should. Yet he has somehow resigned himself to the fact that he has neither the means nor the power to rectify or alter the past. That he is sitting down with me is a testament to his desire to do anything he can and talk to anyone who will listen about his beloved Bogoro.

Seven months later, in August 2002, the village was attacked again, Mugeni continues. Again the attack came from Mbusa's militia, which was linked with the Lendu FNI. The village was once more vulnerable because the Ugandan army had withdrawn from Bogoro to its main garrison at the Bunia airport. The village's only protection came from Lubanga's UPC, which was also based in Bunia and unable to provide effective defense for the scattered Hema villages.

The August 2002 assault by the Lendu was ruthless, Mugeni says, with soldiers entering the village huts and hacking people with machetes. They counted thirty-two dead. He narrows his gaze again, perhaps waiting for me to react. But I am at a loss for words.

According to the ICC investigators, Lubanga's control of Bunia amounted to an anti-Lendu reign of ethnic terror. But when Lubanga lost the support of the Ugandans, who discovered he was working with the Rwandans, the Ugandan army then allied with the Lendu militias, whom they armed and helped to retake Bunia from Lubanga's control.

The drive to recapture Bunia began with the February 24, 2003, attack on Bogoro and, according to ICC investigators, was led by Germain Katanga, known as Simba, the Swahili word for "lion." Katanga, now in ICC custody, emerged as a top commander of yet another Lendu militia, the Force de Résistance Patriotique en Ituri (FRPI). A second Lendu commander was Mathieu Ngudjolo Chui, also now in ICC custody, who had quickly risen in the ranks to become the top commander of the Lendu's FNI militia. Ngudjolo, as he is known, and Katanga began the drive to recapture Bunia in late February 2003 by allegedly ordering their militias to "wipe out" Bogoro.[1]

Armed with semiautomatic weapons, rocket-propelled grenades, and machetes and other hand weapons, Katanga and Ngudjolo's fighters surrounded the village of Bogoro on that early morning in February, awakening the terrified villagers with gunfire. As villagers scrambled out of their huts and homes, they ran into a hail of bullets and flailing machetes. From the screams and shouts of the fighters, the Bogoro villagers knew the attackers were Lendu and the ethnically related Ngiti. The fighters methodically killed anything that moved.[2]

Dozens of men, women, and children were chased down and then shot or hacked to death. Some never made it out of their mud-and-thatch huts, which were set on fire as families huddled inside, knowing a gruesome death awaited if they emerged. Some fled to the school building behind the village, and it became a slaughterhouse, with bodies piled on top of bodies.[3] The hapless villagers' light resistance was easily crushed, and as the smoke and stench of burning flesh drifted in the morning air, Katanga and Ngudjolo reportedly met in the center of Bogoro to celebrate.[4]

IT HAS been common practice by militias and military in eastern Congo to keep the captured women as sex slaves and cooks. The women are abducted during such attacks and repeatedly raped, and some are mutilated and left to die. Some of the women captured at Bogoro were reportedly spared this fate, investigators say, by lying about their ethnicity. They were raped upon capture, then given to the fighters.[5]

Katanga and Ngudjolo are on trial at the ICC in The Hague. At the time of this writing, they are charged with crimes related to the Bogoro attack, including war crimes, crimes against humanity, sexual enslavement, and using child soldiers. Katanga and Ngudjolo have admitted to organizing the attack on Bogoro, saying it was part of a military operation to dislodge the Hema militias.[6]

The ICC trial, however, has done little to dispel the agony that lingers in Bogoro. "They destroyed our village. They killed our people. We ask that justice do its work," Mugeni says. At least 275 villagers were killed that day in February 2003. Mugeni speaks without a hint of anger. His apparent lack of emotion puzzles me, given the area's history of vicious ethnic revenge and retribution. Could his anger have burned itself out?

After the Bogoro massacre, other Hema villages were attacked just as viciously, and many Hema fled the region, some going as far as Uganda, never to return. The Lendu destroyed Hema houses, schools, health clinics, churches, and offices, Mugeni says, and only when the United Nations established an outpost in Bunia along with elements of the Congolese army did a tense truce settle over the region.

"We're very happy [Katanga and Ngudjolo] were arrested," Mugeni tells me.

With the two men in custody at the time we talk, I ask Mugeni what he expects will happen next.

"We are waiting for reparations for what they have done here." In Africa, restitution is critical to resolving conflicts, including war. As difficult as it may be for some to comprehend, even a murder can be settled between families as long as an admission and apology are made and the proper compensation—usually cows or other livestock—is provided to the offended party. Life goes on. There is a certain logic to it: the dead cannot be returned, and starting a revenge war only brings more death.

What does Mugeni expect as restitution?

"It depends on the victims," some of whom have suffered greater losses than others. "Here, where a person kills another," he explains, the resolution is determined by the "point of view of the victim." It can be cows or money.

What if Katanga or Ngudjolo can't pay?

"Then maybe [aid groups] can help," he says.

It dawns on me that Mugeni probably sees me as a vehicle to attract someone with money to help this village. It's understandable, since the destitution of this village is obvious.

One of the villagers sitting with our group, which has grown to a dozen men, nods in agreement about restitution. "We're very poor," he says. "It was not like this before. We had houses and wealth."

"Crimes were committed everywhere," says another. "The conflict was caused by various leaders," suggesting that the region's bloody fighting was not due to ethnic hatred but political leaders making trouble for their own benefit. The man takes a forgive-and-forget attitude. "A man like Germain Katanga is not able to give back what he did here. For us, it is best to forget what happened."

"We have never understood why they were fighting," Mugeni says of the warring militias. Ethnic conflict in the region began to intensify as early as 1998, he says, with the arrival of the Ugandans and Rwandans. Even though there had been wars between the Lendu and the Hema in the past, it was never as bad as it became in the late 1990s, lasting until the Ugandans left in 2003. The first ethnic war was fought long ago, in 1911, Mugeni says, followed by another some fifty-five years later, in 1966. Others erupted in 1981 and 1982, and then again in 1992. But the fighting never lasted, he says. Sides would meet, and things were resolved.

Why is everyone here so accepting of the situation and anxious to forgive and forget? Isn't anyone angry?

One man sitting on a gleaming motorcycle nods. "I'm very angry," says Nestor Kabagambe, thirty-six, because people lost their lives. "They looted my property. I've never understood what the fighting was about. I lost my home, my cattle, and my relatives." Kabagambe lost forty-six cows, two houses, and nine family members who were burned alive inside one of his houses in a neighboring village. Rather than enjoying life as a farmer and cattle herder, he now operates a motorcycle taxi, carrying his fellow villagers around the region.

Bezaler Nzwenge also lost his family to the slaughter in the Bogoro schoolhouse. "My people hid in the school," he says. In the chaos of the February 2003 massacre, many people just ran, including himself, leaving him uncertain of his family's fate. He only knows that he has never seen them again. "Maybe they ran away," he says, gazing at the ground.

Nzwenge found the remains of his father, however. Like others who were shot or killed with machetes as they tried to flee, his body was buried in a shallow grave where it lay. Nzwenge returned to Bogoro in 2004, about a year after the massacre, and as he wandered in the fields behind the village, he saw a piece of cloth covering some partially buried human bones. He recognized his father's shirt. He dug the soil and unearthed a skull. He was shocked as he recognized the pattern of the teeth: it was his father. "We buried just the bones," he says.

Is he angry?

Nzwenge shakes his head no. But he quickly admits, "It's hard to forget. It's true we were rich and had beautiful houses. What happened here left us poor. We have to pay school fees [for children]. But we have no means to do so. We're growing food," he says, but it is just enough to eat, not to sell and make money.

Not all of the violent death in Bogoro was purely ethnic, since the tribal boundaries are often blurred. A Lendu man who has lived in the Bogoro village for many years explains that he lost his family just as his Hema neighbors did. David Binyomwa is sixty-one and has lived among the Hema for most of his life. He lost eleven people in his family in the February 2003 Bogoro attack. His children, nieces, and nephews fled to the village school that became a charnel house. "We've never seen them. I feel sad. I'm suffering. Even my wife was killed." He lost five houses, 160 cows, three daughters, three sons, and his second wife, he explains.

What punishment is suitable for the Katanga and Ngudjolo?

Binyomwa shrugs. "It's a matter [for the] judges."

"This war was very bad," says Onisumu Anyaga, fifty-four. "People had to leave the village, but no matter where you went, they [the Lendu] were chasing you. No one here knows exactly why they were fighting. Only they know all sides were victims." Anyaga lost five children. "They were shot by soldiers," he says. "They [the soldiers] saw people running, and they would stand and shoot you."

Anyaga is not from Bogoro but from a village nearby, Nombe, seven miles to the south. "People ask me why I am here [in Bogoro]." The answer is simple. "I know my family was killed [in Nombe]. I tried to go back with the army," he tells me, but he couldn't face the memories of those he had lost and was afraid he would find their remains. "I still don't want to go back."

Instead, he's rebuilt his life in Bogoro, starting a new family with a woman who survived the massacre. They now have six children, and he repairs radios and bicycles. "We're happy these people were arrested," he says of Katanga and Ngudjolo. "They were the cause of our suffering." When I ask what the ICC judges should do with the accused, he shrugs. "It's up to them."

Mugeni tells me that he and others don't understand why the ICC has only focused on militia leaders from Ituri. "We're angry because only people of Ituri were arrested," he says. "If [the Congolese officials] were arrested, people here would be happy. So many in Kinshasa were involved. Then we would believe the ICC is doing its job well."

What do the villagers think of the ICC?

"The ICC is a world of whites," says Eric Mugisa, twenty-seven, but that's good, because "there is no corruption there." If these militia leaders were tried locally, the corrupt Congolese courts would let the accused go free for just a small bribe. "It would be an unfair justice."

Simon Kabeda, forty, who also lost his family, says that each time he wanders into the cultivated fields surrounding the village, he is reminded of that awful day. More human remains appear in the fields each year, like skeletons emerging from their shallow graves. "We see bones of people and we realize they were killed."

Five years have passed since the massacre occurred, and I suggest that most of the bones probably have been cleared from the fields and reburied by now.

But Kabeda shakes his head. "We're afraid to touch the bones." Not only is there an instinctual revulsion to handling human remains, there is a strong taboo. "It's a psychological problem," he says with a nervous smile. "You may touch the bones and there may be spirits there." Handling the bones could bring trouble, especially if you offend the spirits by not being a relative to the deceased. "You don't know whose bones they are."

The crowd around me has continued to grow. Nearly twenty men have gathered. Yet women suffered some of the worst of the attacks, having been raped, kidnapped, and handed out to soldiers. I turn to a woman who has been lingering at the periphery and listening to the conversations.

Dorolire Nembe, thirty-six, survived the many attacks on Bogoro, which she remembers first began when she was fifteen. She is convinced the only reason she is alive today is because a higher power protected her. "God helped [me] to survive," she says, while so many of her family and friends did not. "We ran away," first taking the road to Kisenyi and then continuing on to Uganda, where she and ten others found a refugee camp with food.

Kezia Bonebana also survived. "It was very sad. We had children with us." She lost six of her own daughters and additional nieces and nephews. "We have nothing to think about," she says of her seemingly empty future. "We lost everything." She looks forward to the punishment of the militia leaders who attacked the village. "We wish that justice can be rendered so peace can be restored. If peace can be restored, that's what is very important for me."

Bonebana has eight children now, and as we talk, a boy about ten years old clings to her skirt. She hugs him and explains that he's the son of village chief Mugeni. The boy is deaf, she says, due to the shooting during the Bogoro attacks. As a result, he does not speak. She squints as the memory brings back painful memories, and nods, acknowledging the boy's problem.

We've been sitting on the stools and benches for nearly two hours, talking about the attacks. As the conversation pauses, the young man, Eric Mugisa, says he wants to show me some of the bones of dead villagers. Most of the group declines to go, having seen them before.

We stop first at the schoolhouse, which still operates despite its poor condition, not to mention the massacre that took place within its walls. It is a stout structure of mortared stone and mud brick. The plaster walls inside are broken and riddled with bullet holes.

Mugisa shows me some crudely formed letters on the wall of one classroom that is no longer used, written in the dried blood of one of the victims of the Bogoro massacre, he says. This was the execution room, and he interprets the words. "This is the first epidemic," they read, meaning that the attack on Bogoro was the beginning of an "epidemic" of ethnic death that would visit the region. One of the fighters had dipped his finger in a pool of fresh blood to write on the wall as bodies were being piled, chillingly predicting that this day was only the first of many meant to wipe out the Hema.

The other classrooms are used every day, and in the one beside this death room, I see the day's lesson scrawled on the blackboard: geometric equations. As gruesome as it seems, the situation gives me hope. Despite the massacre, the survivors are now calculating the perimeter of a rectangle. The people of Bogoro will carry on.

From the school, we follow a narrow set of tracks toward the hill that rises in the distance to a commanding view of the valley. Before we ascend, we turn off the road and into the fields, skirting a section that has been recently plowed by a team of oxen and a hand-guided plow. The soil is dark, rich, and moist. We angle through high grass at the field's edge to a cluster of trees and tangled bushes. Mugisa and his friend Jayson Bahemuka squat and carefully pull back the thick overgrowth. At their feet are bleached white human skulls piled on what seem to be thigh bones, pieces of a human hip, and arm bones. The hollow eye sockets of the skulls are dark and haunting, the teeth revealing the silent grin of the dead, howling from the world beyond.

YOU DO not need to go far into or around Bunia to find evidence of the death and destruction that have become synonymous with the Ituri region. Killing on this scale and with this much depravity must have other, deeper causes than ethnic animosities, I suspect. The Ituri region has vast deposits of gold. One such place is Mongbwalu, the region's richest and most famous gold-mining town. It has been over-run many times by different militias. I go there to see it for myself.

3

GOLD FROM BLOOD

MUDDY STREAMS snake across a gravel riverbed just outside of Mongbwalu, home to one of the world's richest gold mines. About thirty young men, some in knee-deep muck, their bodies slick with sweat under a relentless sun, dig in the mud as others sluice the grit for a flicker of the precious ore. This stream is high in the mountains, about fifty miles northwest of Bunia. Gold and the fight for it have defined life in Mongbwalu for as long as anyone can remember.

After bumping along dirt roads leading north from Bunia, we descend into the valley town of Nizi, where a crowded market forces us to stop. Here one can easily find gold for sale, bags of it, I'm told, dug and processed by many hundreds of independent, artisanal miners who live in the hills. The gold eventually ends up in the world's gold markets, such as Dubai's gold souk, where chains of twenty-four-carat gold drape from gaudy displays and are sold by the gram. Some of the gold goes directly to Europe, human rights groups say, having traced its route from the Congo, through Uganda, then to Switzerland and points beyond.

We thread our way through the market to the other side of town and soon pass through an open gate where the road becomes wide and graveled. We have entered Concession 40, one of three large blocks of land owned by the Congolese government. This parcel consists of about three thousand square miles leased to AngloGold Ashanti, one of the world's largest gold producers, headquartered in Johannesburg, South Africa. The operations here are managed by a subsidiary, Ashanti Goldfields Kilo, headquartered in Kinshasa, and a joint venture between Ashanti Goldfields Kilo, which owns 86.22 percent, and the government, which owns the remaining 13.78 percent. The company has a twenty-five-year renewable lease that gives it exclusive rights to mine gold here until July 2016.[1]

All has not gone smoothly. When the Congo's second war broke out in 1998, Ashanti Goldfields Kilo left, unable to protect the mine. That was because the Ugandan army, which had prompted the return to war, marched directly to Mongbwalu and stayed for five years, controlling the region through proxy militias, at first with the ethnic Lendu, then with the ethnic Hema, and then later with the Lendu again. When Uganda finally withdrew from the region in May 2003, the South African company came back. "Political developments" had made the area safer than it once was, but still "politically sensitive," the company states on its website.

In November 2004, the company deployed a team of geologists and administrators to reopen the mine, supported by an unarmed, private security group around Mongbwalu. Gold mining eventually resumed in January 2005. Despite the dangers and smoldering hatreds in the region, the company says that although "there was an appreciable measure of risk associated with the venture, . . . it was manageable."[2] Profits outweighed the risks.

Whether these security forces truly were unarmed, as the company contends, has been challenged by the rights group Human Rights Watch. The security forces were the ethnic Lendu, the same ones who had conducted well-documented carnage in the region on earlier occasions.

With the situation in Mongbwalu more or less stabilized in 2005, the gold company faced yet another problem: the hundreds of independent miners who prowled the mountains pecking, hacking, scraping, digging, and panning for gold. Called artisanal, the small-scale independent miners—*orpailleurs* in the local French parlance—had filled the void when the gold company left in 1998. The term *orpailleur* comes from the process of pounding the gold-bearing ore into grit by hand, then mixing it with water and mercury. The gold bonds with the mercury, and the liquid is then heated and boiled, leaving a residue of pure gold. The company calls these *orpailleurs* "one of the most significant and multi-faceted community-related challenges" it faces.[3]

The company's concern is well founded, since its workforce is vastly outnumbered by native Congolese. In 2007, only 223 people reportedly worked for AngloGold Ashanti in the Congo: 113 employees and 110 contractors.[4] That is a huge drop from the hordes employed at the site during the mine's boom days of the 1960s and 1970s.

Out of a population in the area of about thirty thousand, an estimated one thousand *orpailleurs* work on Concession 40. The presence of these *orpailleurs* is illegal, because the company has exclusive rights to the gold. It is a delicate and dangerous matter, and the company knows it. "There is an inherent potential for conflict between large-scale operators, such as AngloGold Ashanti, working within a formal, regulated land tenure framework on the one hand, and small-scale miners on the other," the company says. "The situation is exacerbated by the fact that these miners may claim to have an historical entitlement. . . . At the same time, the lack of regulation, ambiguous legislation or a legal framework which is inappropriate for small-scale and artisanal operators (and consequently is not enforced) results in the potential for further conflict to extend to security forces, the police and the state."

AngloGold Ashanti appears unwilling to aggravate the situation, saying that the "government needs to take a lead role in addressing the issue along with both artisanal and large-scale miners, NGOs and development agencies."[5] The likelihood of the government doing anything is slim.

I DON'T have to go far to find the *orpailleurs*. When we entered Mongbwalu, I saw men hunkered down at the side of the road behind piles of white rocks the size of golf balls, smashing them into dust. A short time later, on the other side of town, we stop where a platoon of *orpailleurs* are crawling over a wide gravel riverbed. With Kahorha again as my translator, along with another local as our guide, we scramble across an intricate network of dikes, levees, and muddy sluices. The men are organized into teams, each working a section of the riverbed. It is dirty work. Buckets of muddy gravel are scooped and hoisted from shallow pits, then dumped in sluices, where it is cleaned and readied for processing.

The young men here are working for themselves, of course, not AngloGold Ashanti. What they dig here apparently is not enough to make it worthwhile for the company, but it is more than enough for these men. Chonga Ladonga, twenty-four, tells me that each man generates about a gram of gold per day, which is worth about thirty-five dollars, a goodly sum for a day's work in the mountains of eastern Congo. At this rate, they all know they're not going to get rich, he says, but it is more than enough. "We're just getting a few grams each day. This will help us eat and tend to small needs."

Ladonga and the others don't worry about being driven from the site by the company. "If Ashanti has to chase us from here, how are we to live?" He's been digging gold for over ten years, starting when he was just fourteen years old. But the gold has come at a price, and that price has been the lives of family and friends.

Like most of his fellow gold miners, he's a former child soldier. "War came here and we were obliged to fight. There were [militia] leaders who came here and asked us [to] dig gold for them. They gave us a percentage. When we had to dig, [there was] a big percentage for them and a small percentage for us." But these days, with the warring militias long gone, the miners keep all they produce.

Gold cannot be found as easily as it once was, Ladonga says, especially during the peak war years of 2002 and 2003. Many lives were lost then, but it was a good time to dig gold. "It's a tradition. At times of war, when blood is spilled, then there is more gold here." It is as if the blood draws the gold out of the earth, he says. With the coming of peace, the gold became harder to find. "Now we dig and only get enough for a day. Now there is no gold."

Does he want a return to war so that the gold is once again plentiful?

He laughs and says no. But he and his friends want to improve their technique. "We need someone to organize us. We need to modernize."

AT THE Mongbwalu city hall I find the mayor, or *chef de ville*, Jean-Pierre Bikilisende, in his modest office overlooking the town, a crowded jumble of homes along a narrow road that snakes through the valley. The homes edge up the steep hillsides in a maze of mud and brick topped with rusted metal roofs. Bikilisende is friendly and talkative and explains that when the Ugandans came in 1998, "they wanted only two things: gold and wood. Uganda was not here physically, but they directed people here." These were generally the Lendu militia known as the Front for National Integration (FNI), which controlled Mongbwalu from about December 2002 until about August 2005, he says.

During that time, however, the Hema militia, Thomas Lubanga's Union of Congolese Patriots, took control for a while, using this lucrative resource to buy weapons and garner power. "Most groups were fighting to control the mine sites," Bikilisende tells me. "They came to get money to function." The fighting drove many from the region, which once had a population estimated at fifty thousand, most fleeing to Bunia and Beni, a town farther south, and others going as far as Uganda. "Some are only now starting to come back." Bikilisende also left, taking his family to Butembo, a city south of Bunia, in 2002 and returning in 2004.

Life has not been easy for the returnees. "They have a problem with what they have to do to reestablish [their lives]." With employment at the AngloGold Ashanti mine severely limited, "many people are trying to dig gold." But "digging gold is very difficult. They have to dig very, very deep." Many of the town's residents are too old for the rigors of mining "and have nothing to do. It's a big problem." Crime, drugs, and alcohol are problems, he says with a dismal shake of his head. "If they can get jobs again . . . it will be the solution."

Is there a potential for war?

Yes, it's possible, Bikilisende acknowledges, but so far the region has been quiet. "Those who fought with armed groups are very good. Some are digging gold or making business." Generally, people in Mongbwalu are "talking friendly. Some of them go to the courts to solve their problems." After a pause, Bikilisende confesses that former militia fighters can still be a problem. "Some of the militia [fighters] who committed bad crimes here are not ready to come back. They are not very peaceful."

THE FIGHT over gold in Mongbwalu is a prime example of what lies beneath the smoldering conflicts that have caused millions of deaths across eastern Congo. But rarely are the conflicts spontaneous events arising out of raw ethnic hatred. Outside interests, specifically those of Uganda and Rwanda, have long been aware of how easy it is to manipulate and control eastern Congo. When the Ugandan army took over the Ituri region in 1998 as part of the second Uganda-Rwanda invasion of the Congo, it initially focused on gold mines in and around the town of Durba, in the Haut Uele region north of Ituri, an area about a hundred miles north of Mongbwalu. Durba's gold was much closer to Uganda's West Nile district than the gold at Mongbwalu, which made the cross-border transport of this precious commodity very easy. The area also was beyond the grasp of whoever controlled Bunia.

The plunder did not always go smoothly. In one incident documented by researchers, the Ugandans nearly destroyed a gold mine near Durba in December 1999 when the mine collapsed, killing one hundred miners.[6]

At Mongbwalu, the Ugandans had the local miners dig for gold but required each miner to pay one gram of gold to the militia each day. The rest they could keep. On average, two thousand men mined the concession six days a week, according to reports, producing a total of two kilograms, or 4.4 pounds, of gold each day for the militia commander.[7]

Obtaining the mine was one thing. Keeping it was another. The blood that has been shed at Mongbwalu has been horrific, an unheralded occurrence of human misery prompted by a voracious desire for gold and the guns it can buy. As ethnic militias fought over Mongbwalu, Uganda and Rwanda were in the background, acting like puppet masters wielding control and providing arms and advice.

With the goal of controlling the mine and extracting its gold, in a span of eighteen months, from 2002 to 2003, Hema and Lendu militias, variously supported by Uganda and Rwanda, gained and lost control of the Mongbwalu mine five times. In the process, thousands of civilians were killed, some in brutal street executions with guns, knives, arrows, and machetes. The slaughter forced tens of thousands to flee their homes with nothing but the clothes on their backs.[8]

By early August 2002, already four years into the Ugandan occupation of the Ituri, the Ugandans decided the dominant Lendu militia was becoming too chummy with the transitional government in Kinshasa being crafted by President Joseph Kabila, the son of assassinated leader Laurent-Désiré Kabila. Both Uganda and Rwanda vehemently opposed the government of young Kabila, prompting Uganda into a hasty partnership with Hema militia leader Thomas Lubanga. Lubanga easily pushed the Lendu forces out of Bunia, which opened the door for him to take the biggest prize of all, the Mongbwalu gold mine.

But when Uganda learned that Lubanga had a secret deal with Rwanda, Uganda did an immediate about-face, abandoning Lubanga to his Rwandan backers, and rekindled its partnership with the Lendu militia. According to a confidential report by a UN panel of experts, Rwanda had trained some of Lubanga's Hema fighters in late 2002. Despite Uganda's abandonment, Lubanga was strong enough that he drove north to take Mongbwalu, unwilling to forgo the chance to exploit the gold mine.[9]

But capturing Mongbwalu proved harder than Lubanga had anticipated. The first attack on Mongbwalu, in November 2002, was a miserable failure. Lubanga was given a fresh supply of weapons from Rwanda and found additional troops from a sympathetic militia led by a man known as Commander Jérôme (Kakwavu Bukande).[10] Lubanga's militia went on a rampage, hunting Lendu in the forests around Mongbwalu, catching and killing them at roadblocks.

According to a witness, "The UPC arrived in Pluto [a town near Mongbwalu] at about 9 A.M. . . . . If they caught someone they would ask them their tribe. If they were not their enemies, they would let them go. They killed the ones who were Lendu. . . . The UPC would shout so everyone could hear, 'We are going to exterminate you—the government won't help you now.'"[11]

Another witness said, "A group of more than ten with spears, guns and machetes killed two men . . . in the center of Mongbwalu. . . . They took Kasore, a Lendu man in his thirties, from his family and attacked him with knives and hammers. They killed him and his son (aged about 20) with knives. They cut his son's throat and tore open his chest. They cut the tendons on his heels, smashed his head and took out his intestines. The father was slaughtered and burnt. We fled. . . . On the way, we saw other bodies."[12]

Said another: "Ngabu was a Lendu who couldn't flee. He had lots of children and was trying to carry them. They shot at him. He fell on one of his children and died. Another woman, Adjisu, was shot in the leg. She had her baby with her. They caught her as she was trying to crawl along the ground. They cut her up with machetes and killed her. They cut the baby up as well. Some people were thrown into the latrines. The [Lubanga militia] said they were now the chiefs."[13]

The killings by Lubanga's Hema UPC militia continued through December 2002 and into 2003. One man describes the killing: "I saw many people tied up ready to be executed. The UPC said they were going to kill them all. They made the Lendu dig their own graves. I was not Lendu, but forced to dig as well or I would be killed. The graves were near the military camp. It started in the morning. They called people to quickly dig a hole about four feet deep. They would kill the people by hitting them on the head with a sledgehammer. People were screaming and crying. Then we were asked to fill the grave up. We worked till about [4 P.M.]. We buried the victims still tied up. There must have been about four [UPC] soldiers doing the killing. They would shout [at the victims] that they were their enemies. . . . I don't know how many they killed in total, but I must have seen about one hundred people killed."[14]

Once in control of Mongbwalu, the Hema UPC militia promised gold to all who had helped capture the mine. According to reports, Lubanga's Rwandan backers demanded that gold be sent directly to the Rwandan capital of Kigali. To meet this demand, the Hema realized they needed equipment and mining expertise, neither of which they had. So they ordered the *orpailleurs* to dig, and each miner had to pay a portion of his results to the UPC militia. The militia found that one shift a day was not enough, so it set up nearly round-the-clock mining.

"The workers were not paid," one miner said. "It was hard labor. They had to dig under big stones without machines. They had only hand tools like pick-axes. They were given bananas and beans to eat and they were beaten. Some tried to run away by pretending to go to the toilet. The Hema militia guarded them. As the Lendu had fled, all the other groups were made to dig."[15]

As gold production increased, so did the volume of air traffic in and out of the airstrip south of Mongbwalu, according to investigators. "When the [Hema] were in Mongbwalu they sent their gold to Bunia and from there it was sent to Rwanda. In exchange they got weapons. A number of soldiers told me this," a miner said. "When they were here there were at least two flights per day. The gold was used to buy weapons and uniforms."[16]

The Hema reign over the coveted gold was short-lived, however. The Ugandans, former Hema allies, in November 2002 had forged an alliance with Lendu leader Floribert Njabu. In March 2003, the Hema were driven out of Mongbwalu by the combined forces of Uganda and Njabu's FNI militia.

After chasing the Hema out of Bunia, the Ugandans and the FNI drove north toward Mongbwalu. Just days after retaking Bunia, the

Lendu FNI forces attacked the town of Kilo, near Mongbwalu, beginning a vicious ethnic reprisal against any suspected of collaborating with the fleeing Hema UPC militia. Local residents told Human Rights Watch investigators that at least a hundred people were killed at Kilo, many of them women and children, and shops and houses were looted. Those who survived were forced to carry what was looted. A month later, residents still reported the odor of rotting corpses in the nearby forest.[17]

"At Kilo Mission on top of the hill there were many Lendu combatants," one witness reported. "They had a few guns but mostly machetes, bows and arrows. They were very dirty and had mud on their faces so we wouldn't recognize them. On the hill we saw many bodies of people who had been killed. They were all lying face down on the ground. They were naked. The Lendu were getting ready to burn the bodies. There were many of them, too many to count."[18]

Despite the killing, the Ugandans and the Lendu pushed on, arriving in Mongbwalu on March 13, 2003.

Some two months later, in May, the Ugandan military formally withdrew from the Ituri but left behind their surrogate militia by handing control of Mongbwalu to an FNI commander. Witnesses said that the Ugandan army also left a stockpile of ammunition and weapons. And it was not surprising that several months later, a shipment of Ugandan arms bound for Mongbwalu was seized by UN forces in Beni, a gold-trading town south of Bunia. The men captured with the arms shipment confessed that the weapons were meant for the Ugandan-supported FNI.[19]

But the ethnic fight over the Mongbwalu gold still wasn't over. When Ugandan regular forces had withdrawn from Ituri, the Lubanga's Hema UPC launched another attack on the town on June 10, 2003, and pushed the Lendu FNI out. Forty-eight hours later, however, the Hema militia was driven out in turn by the Lendu FNI, largely because of heavy weapons left behind by the Ugandans.

The two-day war was extremely bloody. Some five hundred people, mostly civilians, were killed. One witness said, "There were too many [to bury] so they just decided to burn them instead. They burned for at least three days. There was a terrible smell in the air."[20]

After retaking Mongbwalu, the Lendu again began to exact revenge, but with a morbid twist. The Lendu launched a witch hunt against the ethnic Hema women in and around the town, accusing those who had married Lendu men of spying for the Hema UPC militia and diluting the Lendu ethnicity by giving birth to mixed-ethnicity children. These women had lived among the Lendu most of their lives. Witchcraft played a role: one witness said, "After the June [2003] attack, the Lendu decided to kill all the Hema women without exception. . . . The Lendu spirit, Godza, told them to kill all the Hema women during one of the Lendu spiritual ceremonies. . . . I couldn't stay while they were exterminating these Hema women."[21]

According to another, "In July women were killed at Pluto and Dego. The strategy was to close them in the house and burn it. More than fifty were killed. Pluto was considered the place of execution for Hema people from Pluto and other places too. They captured the women from the surrounding countryside. They said it was to bring them to talk about peace. They put ten women in a house, tied their hands, closed the doors, and burned the house. This lasted about two weeks, with killing night and day. After that, no more Hema women were left in [our area] and the men were prevented from leaving with their children. They called the women 'Bachafu'—dirty. Sometimes the men would be taken to prison. Suwa's husband was asked to pay $300. They told him they killed his wife, and he had to pay thirty grams of gold [$300] to clean the knife they had killed her with."[22]

THE SMALL town of Pluto is not far from Mongbwalu, where the Lendu and Hema militias clashed. We scale a well-worn path that leads to a small compound of mud houses crowding a broad patio of packed dirt. About two dozen people linger on the periphery as I sit with Kiiza Badja, forty-seven, a quiet and unassuming man of mixed Lendu-Hema ethnicity. Yes, he says, he remembers the purge of Hema women by the Lendu militia. It was methodical and happened at night.

"They were in a group, making a lot of noise, going from house to house," he says of the soldiers. "They were looking for Hema." By then, ethnic killing had become normal. "This was common. When a Hema met a Lendu, they had to kill each other." But it had not always been like this. "People used to live together without problem. Suddenly, people were killing on both sides and didn't know why."

Why didn't the Lendu husbands of Hema women stop their ethnic kinsmen? After all, the women were not a threat.

"The men ran away," Badja says, fearing that they would be killed for marrying Hema women, and they believed the women would be left alone. "But that was not the case. There was nothing they could do. [Militia fighters] were angry when they came." Hopefully, all that killing is in the past, he says. "Now we're calm. For now, it is quiet." He still doesn't understand why it all happened, as if a fog of madness had settled in the mountains. "It's a war that came from very far."

Although Badja has mined gold, he doesn't anymore. "To work with agriculture is better than to mine gold," he believes, because money earned from gold disappears too quickly. With agriculture, you can feed your family.

Is there anger and desire for revenge?

Badja shakes his head silently. I sense that he and the others in the town are mentally and spiritually exhausted by the past killing. "There is nothing else I can do."

Leanne Uzele, thirty-four, lives on the other side of town. Word has spread quickly in this small village, and she is waiting for us in a neatly swept and hard-packed dirt compound nestled on the side of a hill. Uzele has warm eyes and a quick smile and settles into a handmade wooden chair. She remembers the nights of terror when the Lendu militia fighters came for the Hema women.

"They cut [their] throats with a knife in the bush and left them," she recalls. "There was no hope." During the day, families of the victims searched for the bodies, but the vastness of the surrounding forests made the the search difficult. "It was a very bad time." No place was safe. In a sad twist of fate, Uzele explains, her nephew happened to be visiting the village of Bogoro on the day it was attacked in late February 2003, and he was killed. It is the same village that I had visited earlier near Bunia.

The killing included the Hema women's children, Uzele says. "There were many killings here. Even the young boys who were born of Hema women and other women . . . they had to find those children and kill them." Strangely, they left the young girls to live. "It's really sad."

A cloud of distrust and horrific memories lingers over the town, Uzele states. "Life was easy here because of the gold," but that sense of ease and prosperity is gone. Since the fighting has subsided, "People are just now returning. It's a time now to rebuild their lives. Most who come back are involved with the gold because it is easier. Agriculture takes time . . . but gold is very easy and fast." Past relationships are also returning, in which some grow food while others mine for gold. "Confidence has come back. Lendu used to cultivate for Hema. This is started again."

Pluto's mayor, Emil Mbele Bandetena, lives nearby and motions us into his mud-plastered home, where we settle into padded chairs. The walls are decorated with posters that seem wildly out of context: one of Britney Spears and another of Saddam Hussein on trial that proclaims, "He was targeted."

Bandetena tried to convince the bloodthirsty militias to stop the killing, but it only angered them, he recalls. "The Lendu militia called Dracula wanted to kill me. I had asked them to stop the atrocities, so they considered me an enemy." He was forced to flee, he says, walking four days and nights to Lake Edward and eventually making it to Uganda.

"I know of five Hema women who were killed by machetes and bullets," Bandetena says. "[Lendu] accused women of being spies and reporting information on the FNI to the [Hema]." He pauses, lost in thought. "It was not a good time. At that time there was no law. No one could stop them from doing this." He pauses, trying to make sense of it. "The struggle was to control the Mongbwalu mine. The gold promoted war in the region. Lendu commanders took the gold to Beni, and then brought weapons back," he says, confirming the UN special report of the intercepted shipment of weapons from Uganda.

"All the mines were controlled by the Lendu," and it still seems to be the case, he says. "When [AngloGold] Ashanti came, the [Hema] went to the company, but they couldn't go because the Lendu controlled the area. The Lendu said it was now for them."

How that can be, since there is so much independent mining going on all over the area?

"Each community has its own area [to dig gold], like before." Clans have staked their claims and don't want others, including the local government or the gold company, on their parcels. "They don't want to submit to local authorities," he says. After another pause, he offers a chilling prediction: "This may turn into another ethnic conflict."

4

CAULDRON OF CHAOS

————————

A WEEK later, in June 2008, and far south of the gold fields of Mongbwalu, I sit in a sunny room with white plastered walls and a ceramic tile floor. This is the seat of government for North Kivu province, located in a quiet corner of Goma, a town strategically nestled at the top of Lake Kivu and on the border with Rwanda. The room overlooks a large white tent with the distinctive blue stamp of the United Nations. Inside the tent are peace negotiators, militia members, human rights activists, and a few journalists. Those in the tent have been struggling for the past six months to keep a peace deal alive that was signed in late January by the numerous militias that have been fighting in eastern Congo for a decade.

Known as the Goma agreement, the accord is supposed to end the bloodshed in North and South Kivu provinces that has taken an estimated three million lives, mostly due to disease and starvation. Heralded as a milestone for eastern Congo, it has been signed by more than twenty groups and sealed with the signature of Congolese president Joseph Kabila. Yet the fighting has continued almost daily. In all, there have been 190 violations of the peace deal, more than one attack per day, and it is getting worse. What peace exists in the area is due mostly to the UN's seventeen thousand peacekeepers spread throughout the Congo and known by the French acronym of MONUC.

45

The main impediment to peace in the region is said to be the renegade general Laurent Nkunda, whose ethnic Tutsi militia controls a vast swath of land surrounding Goma to the west and north, stretching to the Ugandan border. Nkunda's army is the National Congress for the Defense of the People, known by the French acronym CNDP. Nkunda's army has been tied to the Tutsi government of President Paul Kagame, but Nkunda insists he exists only to defend his people, the ethnic Tutsis born in eastern Congo, from the Hutu militias driven out of Rwanda following the 1994 genocide.

I am with the political leader of a local militia frequently aligned with the Hutus, the Patriotes Résistants Congolais (Patriots of the Congolese Resistance), that goes by the name of PARECO. The group's representative to the peace talks, Sendugu Museveni (no relation to Ugandan president Yoweri Museveni) tells me that Nkunda's forces attacked PARECO units just a week earlier in the mineral-rich Masisi region, some forty miles from Goma. Masisi is Nkunda's stronghold. As Museveni talks, I realize that whatever meaning the Goma agreement may have had when it was signed is quickly evaporating.

Museveni is angry, his eyes flaring, his lips quivering. "The CNDP said they'll withdraw from the peace process. Then, just two days after, they attacked our position. It is war now. If one signatory withdraws from the deal, it is dead. We are waiting for the international community and MONUC. If no solution is found, it is war."

Museveni is convinced that there's an international cabal backing Nkunda's Tutsi militia, which explains why the CNDP seems invincible. It's a conspiracy led by the United States, he says, designed to punish the Hutu perpetrators of the 1994 Rwandan genocide. "All along we have been denouncing the complicity of MONUC and the United States in this process," he rails, making me shift awkwardly in my creaky chair.

I respond that people in the United States only want to help stop the bloodshed, but my remark is ignored.

"They [the United States and MONUC] were present on the day of the peace deal," Museveni continues without a pause. "Since [the agreement] was signed, the CNDP has been fighting and no sanctions have been imposed on the CNDP, even though everyone agreed to stop fighting." Just days after signing the Goma agreement, Nkunda's forces attacked a PARECO village and massacred thirty people, he says. The UN investigated but did nothing, and so Nkunda's forces continued to kill. Museveni offers this as proof of a conspiracy because "none of the killings since have been condemned by MONUC or the US."

There's more. In April, just a couple of months earlier, eighteen people were killed in another village, Museveni says. Children were taken from school at gunpoint by the Tutsis, "but nothing is said about this. There will be no peace with such complicity. There is no chance to reach peace."

Just two months before that, the International Criminal Court had unsealed an arrest warrant for Bosco Ntaganda, the top commander in Nkunda's army, I point out. The thirty-five-year-old Ntaganda, known as the Terminator, commanded Nkunda's forces. The indictment is for crimes that Ntaganda allegedly committed years earlier as top commander for Thomas Lubanga's UPC militia in the Ituri region, a post he held from July 2002 until December 2003. Ntaganda's indictment does little to persuade Museveni. "Why were they waiting all this time?" he asks of the ICC judges, who had secretly issued the indictment two years earlier.

The ICC is relying on the Congolese government to arrest Ntaganda, I explain, but the Congolese refuse to execute the warrant. (The situation has not changed at this writing. Ntaganda has become a general in the Congolese army and still controls the Masisi region.)

Museveni concedes that the indictment of Ntaganda has been a step in the right direction. "If Bosco [Ntaganda] goes to the ICC tomorrow, then Laurent Nkunda would be the next to go."

I suggest that even though Nkunda's CNDP may have withdrawn from the peace process, the talks do not have to collapse. After all, more than twenty militias signed the agreement and Nkunda commands only one.

Museveni shakes his head. "It's not a problem of numbers," he says. Most of the groups that signed the Goma agreement are not legitimate. "Two-thirds of the groups were created during the conference."

They are lining up to get the international funds meant to speed their disarming and reintegration into society. "Instead, some are using the money to recruit soldiers," he says. These groups are called the Mai-Mai, but are simply criminals, he complains. "They have no [military] opponents. They are only bandits from the villages." Because Nkunda's militia is the most powerful, there will be no peace without it. "Since the CNDP has withdrawn . . . nothing is happening."

Museveni returns to his anti-US rant, saying it has always been "a friend to Rwanda. It's the United States that armed [the Tutsis] to take over Rwanda," he says, which empowered the Tutsis to run the Hutus out of Rwanda in 1994. "The same America continues to support Nkunda. Americans have never been for peace. Look at Iraq."

The millions of deaths in eastern Congo are the fault of the United States, Museveni says, who supported the Rwandan army as early as 1996 when Uganda and Rwanda drove Congolese President Mobutu out. The United States helped again in 1998, which prompted what has been called Africa's First World War. "We're sure that all of these wars are enhanced by the Americans. How many more should die before this is called a genocide?" he asks, referring to Nkunda's relentless pursuit of Hutu militias.

Museveni's distaste for Tutsis is clear as he tells me that the Tutsis should be removed from Africa. If the Americans like the Tutsis so much, "give them a state. Take them to your country."

I reluctantly press him about why he's so convinced that the United States is behind the war in eastern Congo. His answer ironically echoes a complaint voiced by his archenemy, Nkunda, who has objected to the wave of contracts that Joseph Kabila's government has been signing with China for everything from mining to construction projects. "The Americans are very angry" since they've been cut out by Kabila. In response, the United States is creating chaos. "That is why they don't want peace here." The war in eastern Congo is purely due to the "selfish interests" of the Americans. In reality, the Chinese are newcomers to the Congo and therefore more visible, while most of the well-established foreign enterprises in the Congo are South African, European, or Canadian.

Museveni returns to the topic at hand. "This is the last chance," he fumes about the crumbling Goma agreement. "We're very tired of responding to the capriciousness of the Tutsis, who do whatever they want because they're supported by the Americans. We will not accept to be dominated all the time by Tutsis."

The Mai-Mai Mongols

The sense of impending doom that permeates my conversation with Museveni dissipates when I meet with one of the major Mai-Mai groups, the so-called bandits that Museveni was complaining about. In many ways, the Mai-Mai have been and continue to be something of a wild card in the ebb and flow of war in eastern Congo, generally acting independently but aligning with the Hutus or others when expedient. Known for their fondness for magic, spirits, amulets, herbs, and potions, the Mai-Mai are the region's homegrown militias, vowing to protect their native villages from the Tutsis and Hutus, both of whom they consider invaders. Félicien Miganda is the political and military coordinator of the Mai-Mai Mongols, and we meet on a terrace overlooking Lake Kivu. Not far away from us a group of Chinese businessmen and businesswomen become increasingly loud as they drink beer. Miganda is optimistic about peace. "The process will work," he says. "There are signs that things will coalesce."

This strikes me as strange, I say, since there have been so many violations of the peace deal. "There are accidents on the way," Miganda says calmly. The day the Goma agreement was signed, he says, "everybody was very happy," because everyone wants the war to end.

So what happened?

When President Kabila signed the agreement, Miganda says, he did not commit the money necessary to support the completion of the process. Many details need to be decided about when, where, and how the militias will stand down so peace can be established. The agreement sets up a framework and a commission that meets daily in the UN tent I saw earlier. But the Congolese government is not paying the food, hotel, and transportation bills of the various militia negotiators.

And Nkunda's CNDP militia is still fighting, I say.

That's easily explained, Miganda responds. "If the CNDP is attacking, it's a means of pressure to force the government to [do] what they promised in the peace process." The sporadic clashes occur because the fighters are hungry and are going after food. The peace process "requires more money than the government can pay. It needs a helping hand," and that hand should come from the international community.

The key to peace in the region lies across the border from the Congo, Mirganda says, in Rwanda. The Rwandan government needs to support the Goma agreement. "We think that if we want a permanent peace in Congo, we should help Rwanda." That means the Rwandan government must settle with the Hutu FDLR. "Finding a political solution to the Rwandan problem" is the first step to a permanent peace. The Mai-Mai groups, he explains, operate largely outside of that central conflict between Rwandan Tutsis and Hutus. The mission of the Mai-Mai is protecting the indigenous villages. "We protect people against any attacks. If we are not attacked, we don't fight."

Tales of a Tutsi

Since the key to peace in eastern Congo seems to be Nkunda's CNDP militia, I sit down with spokesman Rene Abande at one of Goma's better hotels. It is late afternoon, and he and other members of his delegation are sipping South African wine in the shade of canvas awnings. These are not the loathsome fighters who have been described to me. "We're still in the peace process," Abande assures me when I ask why the group has pulled out of the talks. But he quickly adds, "We are not participating in some [of the] talks."

You can't have it both ways, I say.

Abande disagrees. The CNDP is not critical to every step in the process, he says.

What is causing Nkunda to balk at the agreement?

The problem is that until recently, the Congolese government has refused to consider amnesty for Nkunda's soldiers, Abande says, which prevents them from joining the national army. "There is no amnesty until now. It is not possible to mix forces with the government without forgiving them for only the crime of insurrection. It's necessary to give them an amnesty."

Amnesty for Nkunda's fighters, then, has become the major sticking point in the talks. The amnesty that's being offered is only for the crime of insurrection. Nkunda's forces have been fighting for five years, having attacked the South Kivu capital of Bukavu four years earlier, when Nkunda claimed the Hutus were killing his ethnic Congolese Tutsis and planning to reinvade Rwanda. The CNDP was later accused of random killings, rapes, and other atrocities during the short time it held Bukavu. In addition to worrying about his soldiers, Nkunda fears that his top commander, Bosco Ntaganda, could end up like other militia leaders from the Congo who are sitting in The Hague awaiting trial in front of the ICC.

The French term *brassage* is often used to describe the integration of forces that the Congolese army wants. Fighters from various ethnic groups are put in the same units, and tensions rise because former combatants are expected to work together. While it may be good in theory, grudges and wildly different loyalties aren't abandoned easily, and so *brassage* often fails.

Amnesty and *brassage*, however, do not answer the stinging criticism from the justice community regarding the use of amnesty to stop the fighting. Is it right for these soldiers and their leaders to be protected from prosecution even though they stand accused of widespread crimes against unarmed men, women, and children that go far beyond the so-called fog of war? Most human rights activists say no, as do many in the international justice community, who argue that a lasting peace cannot exist without justice. At this time, the UN's special tribunal for Rwanda is hard at work in Arusha, Tanzania. The possibility of establishing a similar tribunal to prosecute those accused of crimes in eastern Congo over the past dozen years has been discussed, but the decision has been put in the hands of the ICC. The sheer scope and number of the crimes committed throughout eastern

Congo makes prosecution an incomprehensible and impossible task. The easiest solution is to grant blanket amnesty, which is about all the Congolese seem capable of. Yet amnesty leaves an already victimized population at endless risk.

Issues surrounding amnesty pale compared to an even larger problem, Abande says: the Congolese government does not truly want peace in eastern Congo. "There is no political will at the high level to make peace. They spent much to show the international community that the CNDP has refused the peace process," for the simple reason that now "they can go back to war."

The government wants war?

Abande nods with certainty. The government has not funded the talks, he says, echoing what I had been told earlier.

So it's all about money?

"That's a sign," he says. In addition, Nkunda repeatedly attempts to open up channels of communication with the Kabila government but is turned down every time. "They just don't want it."

Abande portrays the CNDP as a victim, not the problem. What then, I ask, does the CNDP see as the solution?

His answer is immediate and unequivocal: get the Hutu militia out of eastern Congo. "They must be moved so we can leave our families in peace." As long as the Hutu FDLR militia is in eastern Congo, Nkunda's forces must remain. "What will happen to these [Tutsi] families" if Nkunda's forces are demobilized? Abande asks. "They [the Congolese government] can't answer that."

Once the Hutu FDLR militia is gone, tens of thousands of Congolese Tutsis living in the refugee camps in eastern Congo can return to their lands, Abande says. But the government doesn't want this to happen because as long as there is war, the government can blame it on Nkunda and continue to exploit the area's mineral wealth.

Nkunda's CNDP is not the stumbling block to peace, Abande argues, because the militia is willing to turn over its territories to the government. "The government came to take our places," he says. "We are ready to give it, but it must be done [within] the peace process.

How can this happen if the CNDP won't participate?

"For us, it is a concession to sit at the table." Now the government needs to show its commitment. "If Kabila wants, there will be peace. For me, the cure is there. He [Kabila] is strong, and we are weak. He is heading a nation."

Seething ethnic hatred, distrust, and rivalries run deep. With accusations flying in all directions, peace in the eastern provinces of Congo seems a fleeting fantasy.

Humanitarian Voices

The law offices of Goma attorney Joseph Dunia Ruyenzi are in a quiet, commercial corner of the city, an island of serenity in a sea of turmoil. Comfortable couches face his floor-to-ceiling bookshelves crammed with volumes of law books, papers, and objets d'art. Ruyenzi has been working for peace for the past fifteen years, he tells me. I compliment his tenacity, then ask if peace in eastern Congo is possible.

Ruyenzi shrugs. "It's as if there are parts of this country that don't want to help its people," he says. "When the [peace] process reaches an important height, it falls down."

Continuous involvement of the international community is critical, Ruyenzi says, as demonstrated by all the work done by aid groups in the buildup to the Congo's 2006 presidential election. But after the election, international involvement in the Congo withered and conditions reverted. Without the constant presence of foreign aid groups, eastern Congo "will reach the Somalia situation," Ruyenzi says. "The Congo will be a land for all the terrorists, mafia."

In humanitarian terms, "the Congo problem is more important than Darfur," he says with unflinching conviction.

Christian and animistic eastern Congo are not exactly fertile ground for Islamic fundamentalism, I say, even though eastern Congo is ruled by the gun, much like Darfur.

"A big part of the country is not under the control of the government," he replies, and in reality provides "sanctuaries for armed groups."

Can the Congo dig itself out of the mess?

"Corruption is at the top," he says with a doubtful shake of his head. "There is no justice, no security. Many people don't live in their houses. They can't harvest their crops. There are no human rights. The misery is complete."

Ruyenzi leans forward on his desk and laces his fingers as if in prayer. Goma is rife with rumors that the UN forces are going to leave. It is not a pleasant prospect. "If [the UN] leaves here, it will be worse than Kosovo," he says. "The Congolese army can't stop the armed groups."

The same armed groups I have been talking with control the mines and ore deposits, Ruyenzi explains, which is what funds and fuels the fighting. The government has no control. The region is up for grabs. "The Congo has resources that attract [buyers] who can go with the government or with armed groups," and most go with the groups. Instability is what attracts the Chinese, he charges, who do not demand transparency, respect human rights, or care if the fees, commissions, and profits from minerals are shared by local communities. "The rebels are exploiting minerals. They're sending children into the holes to dig [minerals]," he says. Planes are flying into the region and out, loaded with minerals. "Yet no taxes are left behind."

Though the Goma agreement has been signed, the renewed fighting and threats by Nkunda's CNDP to withdraw from the peace process has left Ruyenzi pessimistic. "The peace process is in danger," he says, because it avoided "pursuing people who violated human rights." As the CNDP demanded full protection from prosecution, rights advocates were pushing for arrests, Ruyenzi says, a position he supports as a member of the Association for the Defense of Human Rights.

"Amnesty without peace is hard to reconcile," Ruyenzi says, arguing that the militias need to establish peace and disband before amnesty can be considered. "Some people committed grave crimes. The government did nothing to say they should be sentenced. This is encouraging people who [are at] war all the time because they know they won't be sanctioned."

Is the peace process dead?

"There is something to save," Ruyenzi insists. The process has already been valuable if only because it "allowed the rebels' leaders to be known." With leaders now visible, focus has shifted to the government, which previously refused to talk with rebels. Peace in eastern Congo "means speaking clearly with neighboring countries and the warlords," he says, and honest conversation with all parties is critical.

International pressure must be put on Rwanda to resolve the Hutu problem, Ruyenzi argues, since the Hutu FDLR militia and the Tutsi CNDP are the core of the problem. If Rwanda allows the Hutus back into the country without retribution, then Nkunda's forces can stand down. "There is no other solution," Ruyenzi says. "The solution is peace. Do we really need another war?"

Despite Ruyenzi's pleas, war will break out again just a couple of months later, and the Goma agreement will die a quiet death. In late August 2008, Nkunda will launch an offensive against the Hutu FDLR and the Congolese forces, and by October 30 his army will surround Goma, sending some 250,000 new refugees into hastily built refugee camps around Goma, which I will visit a year later.

But before I leave Goma in June 2008, I speak to some of the most vulnerable victims of the chaotic and senseless violence perpetrated by the militias. These victims are everywhere in the eastern Congo, which has become the rape capital of the world.

5

AN EPIDEMIC OF RAPE

SHE IS just ten years old and hugs the leg of her counselor, her new best friend, stammering as she tells her story. She wears only a worn, faded T-shirt that barely reaches her knees, and her body shakes with fear. Pink rubber sandals protect her feet from the sharp volcanic rock. Gripped by her terrible memory, she gulps for air.

I'm told her name is Aduke, and I find her at a sprawling rape recovery center in Goma that takes in some of the most damaged victims of the rape epidemic that has spread throughout eastern Congo. Militias intent on crippling communities by brutalizing, disgracing, and humiliating women and breaking up their families have long employed rape as a tactic of war, yet only recently has the International Criminal Court designated rape as a war crime. Despite campaigns by aid groups, the problem has reached epidemic proportions, spreading like a disease from soldiers and militia fighters into the civilian population.

That day, Aduke had done what she was told to do: go to her family's garden in the surrounding forest to hoe the corn and vegetables. She encountered a neighbor returning to the village. The man took her hand, saying, "let's go back home." She complied, unable to challenge this man despite her parents' orders to go to the garden. He carried her to the bushes, put her on the ground, held her by the neck, and pried apart her legs. "He asked her not to cry, and began to have sex with her," says the counselor, translating Aduke's faltering words. "When he finished, she couldn't walk." So the man carried her on his back and dropped her off at her family's hut, telling her parents that she had become sick. "She couldn't explain to her parents what had happened."

The counselor is Devote Musafire, a chiseled and confident woman wearing a brightly colored dress and headscarf. She gently encourages Aduke to recount her tale, convinced that the process will help heal the wounds that will scar the young girl for the rest of her life.

Musafire is the thirty-six-year-old chief counselor at Hope in Action, a Swedish-funded aid organization affiliated with the Community Pentecostal Church of Central Africa. Victims arrive at the rape centers in Goma after being rejected by family and friends as if they're to blame for what has happened to them. A thin layer of smoke from cooking fires drifts in the air. As with all of Goma, this center has been built on the black lava rock that spews from the flanks of the nearby volcano. It is a rugged and dismal place, and the atmosphere is crushing.

It did not take long for the truth to come out about what had happened to Aduke. Two days after her rape, an infection developed. "When her mother noticed the infection, she had [Aduke] sit in the stream," Musafire explains, her mother thinking that the problem would clear. "It didn't stop," Musafire says, and consequently "she suffered a lot." After ten days, crippled from the searing pain of her festering wound, Aduke finally told her mother what had happened.

The family was outraged and the neighbor was promptly arrested. Aduke's father was a soldier and "was very angry and wanted to kill the man," Aduke says. He tried to bribe a guard to let him kill the man in the jail, but was unable. Aduke does not know what became of the culprit. "I'm really angry with him," she confesses. "I wish he could be killed."

Knowing that life in the village will be impossible for his daughter, Aduke's father brought her from their home about sixty miles west of Goma to this center where she's been for the past week. Aduke remains perplexed and distraught, yet she understands that her life will never be the same. "I cannot go home," Aduke says weakly. "I wish I could stay here." She can for a while, Musafire says with a nod, but when the counselors think Aduke can cope with her new life in Goma, she will go live with her relatives in town.

What kind of future does Aduke face?

Musafire shrugs.

Aduke typifies the legions of rape victims these centers see daily. "When they arrive, they're afraid and are ashamed to go back home," Musafire says. "Villagers know they've been raped."

Rejection by family and friends is a baffling reality, she agrees. First, the woman's self-esteem needs to be rebuilt. "She fears to lose her personal [identity]" because she is no longer the woman she was and is stigmatized for having been raped. The women are counseled, "Even if you were raped, you are still the same. You can go on and take care of your family."

Yet the rape victims face severe social barriers. "Their husbands say, 'I can't take you back,'" Musafire explains. "They come here. So what are we going to do with them? They are very weak, unstable." Some of the women shout and scream at night, the aftereffects of mental and physical trauma. Does the counseling help? Musafire nods hesitantly.

I look around the compound and wonder. These women have fled the thousands of militia fighters who are normally accused of committing the rapes, but now they must flee their own neighbors, who are also raping, the very ones who should be helping them get back on their feet.

How did the situation get this bad?

Most of the rapists are government soldiers or militia fighters under the control of either Tutsi or Hutu commanders, Musafire says. Some perpetrators are the homegrown Mai-Mai militias, and still others are the Congolese police, said to be worse than the criminals they're supposed to control. Some rapists are cattle and goat herders who roam the region. In Aduke's case, it was her next-door neighbor.

Rape is a tactic intended to destroy communities suspected of being enemies of militias, Musafire explains, and now, with civilians committing these acts, the result of a total social breakdown brought on by war.

Why is rape so pervasive when each of the perpetrators has a mother and most likely brothers and sisters? The perpetrators must certainly know the consequences of what they are doing, I say.

"They're away from their families," Musafire says. "They behave like animals. Some men do it to destroy," especially if they were part of an ethnic militia bent on punishing another ethnic group. Sometimes there's simply no clear reason for it. The man who raped Aduke had two wives and certainly was not lacking for sex partners. "Nobody can understand what is in their minds."

Musafire admits that the Congo's hopelessly corrupt court system is a big factor. Soldiers in particular enjoy protection from the courts and police, because their commanders prevent soldiers from being arrested no matter how hideous the crime of which they've been accused. Rape has spread throughout society because men can get away with it. No one is going to do anything about it.

"There's impunity," Musafire says. "They know they can rape and nobody is going to stop them. Nothing will happen. We don't know if they know it's a crime."

How can they not know? I ask.

"They're aware it is a crime, but they also know there is impunity."

The solution, Musafire says, is to turn the tables on the rapists. "The first thing is to stigmatize them" rather than the victims. But before that can happen, the Rwandese militias, both the Hutu and Tusti, "must go home. Militias have to be disarmed."

THE OFFICE of Françoise Kahindo, director of the aid organization called the Union for Life Against HIV, is on a busy street in Goma. I knock on a heavy, unmarked door that opens into a cramped and dark office. Kahindo's mission is to educate her Congolese neighbors about the scourge of AIDS that is so closely linked with rape, a connection that would seem hard to miss. But it is, Kahindo explains, due to the pervasive denial that rape and HIV infections are problems. Just as rape itself is not openly discussed, neither is the spread of AIDS. "If we keep silent, many others will be affected," she says. "There is a connection, that's why we've combined programs" that address both rape and HIV.

The region's rape epidemic is due to the many armed groups entrenched there. "Some are raped by soldiers, other by civilians." Women are victimized because they're the ones who cultivate gardens, collect firewood, fetch water, and travel to markets. The militias set up roadblocks randomly, she says, and "they arrest you and rape you. The problem is war."

Since peace negotiations are still alive when I meet with Kahindo, I ask if she feels optimistic about them. She shakes her head. "It changes nothing," she says of the fragile Goma agreement. "The number of fighters has diminished, but the troops are still in position. So when people have to go out for food or trade, that's when they're raped. Now [rape] has extended to the rest of the [civilian] community. We don't understand what's in the mind of [rapists]."

Much like the code of silence and impunity that surrounds rape, deep-seated and crippling beliefs fuel the spread of AIDS. "Some people think that if he has HIV, and if he has sex with a young girl of two or three, they can be cured," Kahindo says. While she struggles to dispel that misconception, she also fights the idea that AIDS was brought to the Congo from outside. The common belief is that "it started with the invasion from other countries where HIV was more prominent," referring to the invasion of eastern Congo by Rwandan and Ugandan soldiers in 1996 and again in 1998. "HIV is like a fire. It spreads quickly." But the spread of the disease is not always by forced sex. Poverty and desperation forge dangerous alliances. "Many young girls befriend soldiers, due to poverty," she says. "This contributes to the HIV spread."

Victims of the rape epidemic are doubly hurt, Kahindo says. "They suffer two times. First shock is the act itself. The act of rape. The second shock is being a victim of HIV." The problem affects all ages. "It touches all women. From the young up to [those in their] sixties. Some are mutilated with a knife. [In] one case a woman had to have three surgeries" before she was healthy enough to live on her own.

Lives are destroyed. "Women are rejected by their family and relations and [she] finds herself alone. There is a stigma. They are not accepted once they've been raped." It is a crippling and complex problem, she says. "People ignore the facts. They only see a woman who's been raped. There is a cultural problem. Once a woman has had sex with someone who is not her husband, she cannot be married anymore. We try to explain that they are victims and life should continue. It's a part of healing."

The rape problem is more widespread than most are willing to admit, Kahindo says. No one knows how many women have been raped, although some statistics suggest that the number is in the hundreds of thousands. Because of the stigma, many women don't report their sexual assaults. "Most cases of raped woman don't admit it. They keep silent."

The Congolese parliament has recently reformed the country's rape laws, I note, and now requires that specific procedures are followed to ensure the prosecution of rapists. The reforms are supposed to raise awareness that rape is a crime that needs to be punished.

Kahindo doubts that the reform is an effective solution, because prosecuting rape is expensive and time-consuming. "People are disgusted with the law. Once someone has been a victim and goes to court, she's asked to pay money each time they go to court. They get tired of it and don't go."

Although Kahindo agrees that reforms have increased the punishments for rape, she says they're not enforced. Rape suspects are arrested and released, even after conviction. This is a huge disincentive for people to report rape or try to prosecute it. "This affects victims."

Since most rapes are never reported, "very few cases are effectively recorded," which thwarts prosecution before it can begin. Rape victims are required to be examined by a doctor or medical provider who must verify that a rape has taken place. This is also a stumbling block because "most women who are raped in a village don't have access to health care and are without roads or access to the outside world."

Those who can travel must then confront the militias that control the roads and countryside and who may be the same ones responsible for the rapes that have been reported, Kahindo says. "If they're in the bush, they're committing crimes," she says of militia fighters and government soldiers. "How can the international community not take them out of the bush? I can't believe the international community can't neutralize them. When there is peace, all this will end."

Kahindo asks me to follow her through the dark maze of chairs and desks that is her office and into the sun-baked street clouded with roiling black dust and the noise of honking cars. Through another door we enter a spacious room with a cluster of chairs haphazardly arranged on a concrete floor. She introduces me to Honorine Kavugho, a somber woman wearing a gray skirt and a floral blouse. She has a careworn look and the eyes of someone who has suffered.

Kavugho was captured by soldiers and raped repeatedly, then learned she had contracted AIDS, Kahindo explains. Kavugho is waiting to talk to a meeting of regional aid groups fighting the rape and AIDS epidemics. The meeting is in an adjacent conference room, and she hopes that her personal story can convince them to redouble their efforts.

Kavugho was thirty-three at the time of her rape, the mother of seven children. She was on her way to Butembo, a commercial and gold trading town north of Goma, where she intended to do some business with the $2,500 in cash that she carried. She and some thirty others were riding in one of the many commercial trucks that carry both cargo and people.

"We met some soldiers," she says. "Soldiers were hiding in the bush and below a bridge." The soldiers jumped out as the truck approached, firing automatic weapons at point-blank range. Within minutes, many of the passengers were dead or dying. She survived the attack but was grabbed by the soldiers along with another woman. "They took us to the bush [where] we spent four days. They took our clothes and money. They stabbed me in my neck and stomach." She pauses to show me her scars.

She spent most of this nightmare screaming and pleading with her captors. "[I] cried so much [my] voice went hoarse." It didn't matter to the soldiers, she says, who took turns raping her over the course of four days. The soldiers were part of the Hutu militia, she says, the FDLR. Finally, the commander ordered her release "so she could die at home."

Kavugho returned to Goma to yet another tragedy. "When I came home, my husband rejected me and my family. I didn't know if I was still alive." She looks at me with wet eyes that alternate between anger and fear. "All my life has been anger," she says. When she began the trip, she felt like she was on top of the world, but her life quickly turned to misery. "Today I starve. I have to knock on doors to feed my children."

Why didn't her husband take care of the children?

Kavugho shakes her head. "He said he would never share anything with [me] ever again. He called me the wife of a soldier, of rebels, of criminals. If you want, you can go to court."

Kavugho became pregnant as a result of the rape and gave birth to a girl. "The child is suffering," she says, because of her poverty. And so are the rest of her children, the oldest being seventeen. "Now they [all] are starving. I am very sad. My family has rejected me, as if I killed a man. I tell my children that in life there is no hope. You have to take care of yourself. You have to do what you can."

THE RAPE epidemic in the eastern Congo defies description and explanation. Could it be due to a permissive and fatalistic attitude, I wonder, or more likely a complete breakdown in social values? I am reminded of a statement I read months earlier by a military commander who claimed that neither he nor his soldiers had realized that rape was a crime. Only when aid groups and social and health organizations in Goma began to complain about the proliferation of rape did the problem become apparent, the commander had claimed. How could rape not be considered an act of violence? Didn't each rapist have a mother and possibly a sister or two, and wouldn't they be outraged if their family had been attacked? Was it so difficult to view rape as repugnant if the roles of victim and perpetrator were reversed?

I ask these questions of Pastor Clement Lembire, the leader of the New Song Church in Goma. "The [rape] problem is complex here. There are so many factors. They are aware that it is not good," he assures me. "We are conscious of this problem." Lembire encourages his parishioners "to pray for [help against] HIV and sexual violence, because they are really epidemics here."

Lembire sits back and looks at me over a cluttered desk. He says that rape is "a new phenomenon here because of repeated wars. We've learned that one community can humiliate another community." Because of prevailing beliefs and taboos, an effective tool "to humiliate another is to rape his wife and daughters. Armed men rape your wife and mother and it's done publicly." At that point, the damage has been done, he says. The family has been destroyed because of the stigma of rape. "How can you sit and eat with these people?" a husband will ask himself. "The family unit is gone. Even yourself. You are dead."

Doesn't the threat of arrest act as a deterrent?

"Some are taken to prison, but it changes nothing," Lembire says, shifting uncomfortably in his chair. The rape problem is not unique to the eastern Congo, he says, explaining that neighboring Kenya had a wave of violence following the disputed election. Clashing ethnic groups "also used sexual violence during the conflict. Although people know that sexual violence is wrong, they do it anyway."

The solution is prayer, he says.

While I can admit prayer is probably useful, how does it help in cases of rape?

"Through prayer," he says, rapists ask for God's help to "leave the wrong side and turn to the right side."

But why is rape so widespread?

"Africa in general and the Congolese in particular are emotional." Africans tend to act first, and "think after," he explains. "We're more involved in emotions."

After a pause, he adds, "We're a sacrificed generation." During the region's decade of war, "we had no time to think about the future of the nation or our families." Those in their midtwenties to midforties who now have the responsibility of leading the country have known nothing but war; the prevailing norms of a civil society have been suspended for so long that most people know only a culture of violence and the rule of the gun. "That is a serious problem in our generation," but religion can fill the moral void, Lembire claims. "What people need to hear must come from the word of God."

If the law can't combat rape, I ask, what about revenge? Don't those who rape fear that the victims' families will come after them?

Lembire shakes his head. "The population is passive," he says. "A Congolese fears death, so [he] won't fight or criticize for fear of revenge."

I find that hard to believe and say that revenge is a very strong motive and has nothing to do with ethnicity or nationality.

Lembire shrugs. "War created hatred. I [have] worked during a difficult period."

Lembire claims he has been harassed for his attempts to bridge the ethnic divides in eastern Congo, having invited all people to his church. "We prayed together and tried to work out conflicts. It's difficult to reach positive results." For his attempts, "I was menaced by one group or another for betraying one group or another."

The harassment has been subtle, Lembire says, but the message is clear. It came in power cuts to his church, though he paid his bill on time. "They said I was bringing Rwandans here . . . to fight with our country." But it doesn't stop him. "I told people not to return evil for evil."

IF THERE is a way to reverse the rape epidemic, I suspect it may be through the law, which leads me to Christine Mpinda of Dynamic Women Jurists, a nonprofit group of young lawyers struggling to bring rapists to trial and put them in prison. It is an uphill battle despite the recently adopted reform of rape laws.

The old rape statute needed a better definition of the crime, Mpinda tells me, so the new law expands the definitions to include forced prostitution, sexual mutilation, forced marriages, bestiality, sexual harassment, slavery, HIV transmission, and forced pregnancy. It also includes sexual contact with any part of the victim's body.

The law now requires that victims contact police within two days of a sexual attack, Mpinda explains. A doctor must then certify that a rape has occurred, and if so, the victim has the right to treatment from a physician and psychologist. The responsibility then moves to the local prosecutor, who must process complaints and rape reports within one month of receiving them. Rape cases must go to trial within three months of the charges being filed. Once a trial begins, victims can appear in public or in private at court.

Another critical improvement to the law is that soldiers can be arrested without the approval of their commanders, she explains. The protection afforded to soldiers by their commanders has been one of the biggest problems behind the rape epidemic. Along with looting, rape has been a reward for soldiers who capture enemy villages.

Such a practice will be hard to change, since soldiers are not paid or are underpaid, I suggest, and commanders are undoubtedly unwilling to relinquish control of their soldiers to a prosecuting attorney.

Mpinda agrees, saying that it will take time for the effects of the law to take hold in society. "It is true the law exists, but it's true everything doesn't go well." Many rapes go unreported, not only because of the social taboos but due to the complexity and costs of rape prosecution. This is why her group offers free legal services.

Most of the rape cases come out of the Masisi region, she says, which is where Laurent Nkunda's Tutsi CNDP militia controls vast sections of mineral-rich land and routinely clashes with government forces and ethnic Hutu militias.

Prosecuting rape is slow and tedious, because only one court currently handles the cases in Goma. Since Masisi is about sixty miles to the west, "the distance doesn't enable victims to have access to legal help. Most of the [victims] can't pay to travel from their village to Goma." She and the other lawyers accept three cases a month, and each costs from $500 to $1,000 to prosecute.

Ensuring that the process is completed properly is the group's main objective, Mpinda says. Prosecuting each case carefully is very important, since precedents are being set for the future.

"There is a misunderstanding about sexual violence among people as well as judges," Mpinda confesses. Some judges believe that women bring the problem on themselves. "That is a serious problem," even among government prosecutors, and it has made obtaining convictions harder than necessary.

Yet there have been successes. Of the twenty or so cases filed by the group from April through December 2007, twelve resulted in sentences ranging from five to twenty years in prison. The other eight resulted in convictions, and the culprits were awaiting sentencing.

Another problem is compensation for the victims. Although civil penalties are awarded in these cases, the convicted rapists have no means to pay the required compensation. "They have nothing, so they can't pay," Mpinda says, and that problem can only be solved by a general economic turnaround.

In the meantime, Mpinda and the other lawyers in her group are visiting schools to talk about rape as a crime, hoping that by taking the issue directly to children, new attitudes can be instilled in the coming generation that reject rape as acceptable behavior. They also hope to dispel the code of silence among women who won't admit that they've been raped due to the social disgrace.

More women seem to be warming up to the need for better reporting of the problem, Mpinda says. She recently worked a case in which forty women told authorities that they had been raped in a village in Rutshuru district. But due to the panic, confusion, and darkness, the women didn't know exactly who had committed the assaults, only that they had been raped by soldiers. It was frustratingly impossible to bring the case to court, she says, but it also illustrated how pervasive the practice is among all who wear uniforms, competing militias as well as the government forces.

I leave Mpinda's office with a vague sense of hope, knowing that someone is fighting back.

6

THE AGONY OF ABYEI

H OPE FADES, however, when I leave Goma and the realities of eastern Congo begin to sink in. Four years before I ever thought about working in Africa, I spent most of a year in Afghanistan. Despite the medieval mentality that throttles Afghan society with its brutal variant of Islam, life there has a certain logic. There is a system, however archaic. In contrast, abuses and atrocities in eastern Congo lack a rationale, or so it seems.

At the time I am working in The Hague, Netherlands, focusing on the International Criminal Court's trials of African militia leaders from the region. I work with journalists from East Africa who file in-depth stories from some of the region's most troubled areas for the website of the Institute for War & Peace Reporting. Traveling between East Africa's simmering war zones and the tidy, rain-soaked streets of The Hague is often a jarring contrast. From the high-rise offices of the ICC, the world dispenses the justice it thinks is needed for eastern Congo, Uganda, and more recently Sudan. But increasingly, the ICC seems to be treating a symptom, not providing a cure for a pathology that has infected not only the Congo but other countries and continents as well. There's something sinister in eastern Congo, and arresting random militia leaders is not getting to the heart of the matter.

In late 2008, I am on my way to Juba, the sprawling and gritty capital of the semiautonomous South Sudan. I am headed there to present a workshop for local journalists about the workings and purposes of the ICC after two Sudanese were indicted by the court for war crimes related to Darfur. One was a ranking cabinet member in the government of President Omar Hassan al-Bashir, and the other was a commander of the feared *janjaweed* militia, the devils on horseback who have been torching and massacring villages across Darfur.

The ICC chief prosecutor, Argentine attorney Luis Moreno-Ocampo, has just asked the court to indict President al-Bashir for crimes of war and genocide in Darfur. The court mulls the request, which it will later grant without the charge of genocide. Two years later, in mid-2010, it will finally add genocide to al-Bashir's indictment. By asking the court to bring charges against al-Bashir, Moreno-Ocampo ignites a firestorm of controversy. The court's first indictment of a sitting national president raises profound questions about the reach of international law.

I have been in Juba before, in July 2006, during the launch of peace talks between Ugandan rebel group the Lord's Resistance Army and the Ugandan government.[1] Since 2006, the peace talks have devolved into a farcical thrashing of the international community's ardent desire to end twenty years of bloodshed in northern Uganda.

Prior to the launch of the talks, the Lord's Resistance Army decamped from northern Uganda and southern Sudan, settling in the Garamba National Park, once a Belgian colonial hunting ground in the remote northeastern corner of the Congo. The peace talks progressed haltingly as a revolving cadre of rebel negotiators collected tidy bundles of cash for just sitting at the table. Periodically the negotiators would travel to Nabanga, a jungle camp on the border of the Congo and South Sudan, claiming the need to consult with rebel leader Joseph Kony, who trekked from his jungle redoubt with about a hundred of his most hardened child soldiers. Kony commanded five hundred or so fighters and at least that many abductees, mostly women and children. The international community supplied Kony's army with food to keep it from looting, killing, and raping the hapless villagers in and around the park. But that strategy didn't work.

For much of 2008, Kony had been circling his fighters through the very remote regions of western South Sudan, the eastern Central African Republic, and northeastern Congo, looting and leaving a wake of death and destruction, kidnapping hundreds of people and forcing them to carry the stolen food and supplies despite the fact that he was also being supplied by the international community. Some of the kidnappees were kept as soldiers to bolster the army's ever-dwindling ranks due to death and desertion. The raids revealed the former Ugandan rebels for what they were: a vicious militia intent on its own bloodthirsty survival.

Throughout its twenty-year war back in northern Uganda, the LRA had claimed it wanted to overthrow the government and establish a society based on the Ten Commandments—an absurdity since the rebels routinely violated each and every one. Their primary victims had not been the Ugandan soldiers they claimed to be fighting but their own ethnic Acholi tribe, on whose behalf Kony claimed to wage his war. Now, far from Uganda, the rebel army's reason for existing was lost. The army attacked anyone they encountered on the road or in the forest and savannahs. They were just killers, nothing more.

Kony and his army also were masters of manipulation. Throughout 2008, his followers claimed repeatedly that Kony would sign the peace agreement that had been negotiated more than a year earlier, and presumably then he would disband his army. Twice in the spring of 2008, a swarm of international, UN, Ugandan, and other African officials descended on Nabanga for a signing ceremony. Kony never showed. After one humiliating no-show, word spread that the LRA negotiating team and its leader had virtually no contact with Kony, and the rebel master was probably unaware he was to sign the document.

I learned on the eve of my trip to South Sudan in November 2008 that the saga was far from over. The international community again scrambled as LRA negotiators insisted that Kony would sign the agreement this third and final time. As I climb into the small plane to fly from the Ugandan capital of Kampala to Juba, I find myself sitting beside a man dressed in a flowing white robe and skullcap. He

looks familiar. I realize he is Sheikh Musah Kahlil, leader of the Muslim community in northern Uganda, whom I interviewed a couple
of years earlier. Kahlil is one of a dozen northern Ugandan digni-
taries being whisked to Juba and on to Nabanga for the signing. I
reintroduce myself and ask if he thinks Kony will show up. He looks
at me with a wary grin, shakes his head doubtfully, and shrugs. We
engage in light conversation, and it becomes clear Kahlil has little
to say and is largely along for the ride. I can't really blame him. We
part company on the tarmac at the sun-scorched Juba airport as the
northern Ugandans amble toward another plane that will take them
to the jungle.

The potential signing of a peace deal has become such pressing
news that I am forced to postpone my workshop in the ICC. Most of
the South Sudanese journalists are following this latest turn of events
because South Sudan stands to gain nearly as much from a peace as
Uganda, since the rebels have plagued South Sudan as well. I too am
eager to write about the signing, but my efforts to get to Nabanga fail.
The entourage has few seats for the press, and I am not going to be sitting in one of them.

So I turn my attention elsewhere, remembering that six months
earlier, when I was in Bunia in eastern Congo, fighting had erupted
far to the north of Juba along the border between Sudan and South
Sudan, fighting over control of Abyei, a town in the heart of Sudan's
oil-rich region. Control of the oil meant possibly billions of dollars in
revenue for the victor. I had encountered the same situation in eastern
Congo, only this time the mineral was oil. I head for Abyei.

Swamps and Deserts

It's surprisingly wet in South Sudan, a fact that clashes with my notions
of Sudan as I roll north from the regional capital of Wau toward Abyei.
Marshes cover the land, a product of the unruly rivers crisscrossing
South Sudan, in particular the Nile. Cattle roam wherever it is dry. Just
outside of Kwajok, a town well north of Wau, gangly storks poke and

splash in the shallows for fish, frogs, and other aquatic morsels. Occasionally men and boys cast nets from the road's edge. On the opposite side is bone-dry desert.

With me are two Dinkas, both of whom have spent years outside Sudan. The driver is Arik Kuol, thirty-nine, who fled the fighting in the south years ago to attend high school in Khartoum only to be yanked out of school by the Sudanese army and sent to the southern front. "I had to fight my own people," he says bitterly. "There were bullets in front of you and one behind you if you didn't fight hard."

Kuol escaped to Egypt with a tourist visa and refused to return, obtaining immigrant status, which allowed him to stay and study electronics. Kuol eventually secured a scholarship to Canada, and his first job there, he recalls with a laugh, was shoveling snow for retirees and shut-ins. He had only seen snow on television, "and there I was shoveling it." He found work in an electronics factory crafting components for US military weapons systems.

After eight years, Kuol returned to South Sudan, "because our country needs us," he says of the South Sudanese diaspora. He came back to ensure that the semiautonomous South, which won its status in 2005 after more than twenty years of civil war with Sudan, will survive what he fears will be an Arab Sudanese invasion of his homeland. Such an invasion will be resisted to the last man, he vows. "The Dinka are like a rock. If the Arabs destroy the rock, then all of South Sudan will be Islamic. . . . But the Arabs will never be here . . . only if all the Dinka are gone."

Such an invasion is unlikely, I suggest.

But Kuol shakes his head to disagree and reminds me of the freshly built airstrip that he insisted I see west of Kwajok. He said it was being built by a Sudanese company. It could be strategic in any invasion by the north. "Let them come," Kuol says. "We will fight."

Given the ethnic animosities that permeate the south, a united front against the north might be easily broken, I say.

The Dinka and the Nuer, both large tribes in South Sudan, are traditional enemies, Kuol agrees. "They will love each other for half a day and fight the rest of the day. You can never be friends with a Nuer for two days." If the south were invaded, however, the two groups would put aside their differences. "There is a time to fight, and a time to think about the future."

While people in the region are well aware of the value of oil, it is not the most important thing to the Dinka. First and foremost are cows. The Dinka have more words for cows than any other people. "They describe the beauty of cows like no other people," Kuol says, smiling broadly. As if to prove it, he occasionally stops to chat with cowherds about their animals, which often block the road. A good bull costs over $500. Kuol points out the elaborate notching of the cow's ears to mark ownership. The tribal name Dinka comes from an English variant of their word for "cowboy," he says.

The Dinka are Nilotic people numbering more than two million, making them the region's largest ethnic group, inhabiting about a tenth of Sudan. The Nile River floods the grasslands from May to October and recedes from November to April, setting in motion annual migrations that have taken place for millennia. The rivers and swamps divide the Dinka into some twenty-five independent groups governed by lineages. The Dinka call themselves the Monyjang, which means "the man" or "the husband of men," and are generally convinced of their superiority to all other tribes.

It is not unusual for Dinka clans to sacrifice animals to the mysterious gods of the Nile to ensure the tribe's welfare, Kuol says. He's seen and experienced it himself and is quite convinced of its usefulness, despite his heightened skepticism gleaned from years in North America. His village was struck by a strange disease, he says, so the villagers sacrificed a cow to the river. Succumbing to his doubts, he tried to keep the cow from drowning by pulling it out the water with its lead rope. But the villagers warned him, "If you don't let go of the rope, you will disappear too, never to be seen again." He looks at me with frightened eyes, then insists that his village was cleansed of the disease after he let the cow disappear into the river.

We pass dozens of fishermen hunkered down at the roadside with their wispy fishing nets and reed baskets, and occasionally I spot a large drum hanging from a tree in the midst of a clearing. This is where the Dinka gather to dance at night, Kuol explains, lacking other forms of entertainment and opportunities to socialize. "They cannot go anywhere," he says with a shrug, because their main means of transportation is walking.

After six hours on the road, we reach Agok, the town where most of the fifty thousand people of Abyei fled from the onslaught of Brigade 31, part of the Sudanese armed forces, six months earlier, in May 2008. We stop at a quasi-military camp to ask directions, and Kenyi, my other companion, a translator and guide, erupts into an argument with a sergeant who threatens to arrest us for illegally entering a military post. It's an absurd charge, since the camp is neither marked nor fenced. Afterward, when I question the wisdom of challenging the army, Kenyi tells me not to worry, since he has a commission in the South Sudan army. He assures me that he'll explain later, but even so I suspect I may be in the company of more than just a friendly translator.

Bombs over Abyei

We stop at a whitewashed structure surrounded by swept dirt and a wire fence, parking in the shade of leafy trees that provide scant relief from the relentless Sudan sun. This is the area's seat of government, I'm told, as we pause to watch several hundred cows trailing a man beating a hand drum, a practice that Kuol explains is an ancient and very efficient way to herd cattle.

In the cool darkness inside, I meet Joseph Dut Paguot, the ranking government official in Agok. He is a somewhat diminutive man with a leathery face who sits behind a sprawling desk flanked by the flag of South Sudan. "We've been fighting [over Abyei] from here" since 1994, Paguot explains, making the community more of a military base than a seat of local government. But this is a good thing, because "most of the people of Abyei fled to this area during the war" just six months earlier. "We were ready here to receive them. Some have tried to go back to Abyei" but have been unable to reestablish themselves. "The future situation is not good," but "it is better than before." Hatred lingers because about two hundred people were killed in the May 2008 attack at Abyei, he says.

The May attack was the latest in the long-running dispute over the border between Sudan and South Sudan, Paguot explains. It will be somewhat settled, however, just half a year after my meeting with Paguot, when in July 2009 the Permanent Court of Arbitration in The Hague rules that the disputed boundary is about halfway between the two different boundaries claimed by the south and north. Sudan's boundary had been drawn south of Abyei, and South Sudan's desired boundary had been drawn far north of Abyei. In dispute, of course, are the vast oil fields on both sides of the border. But the question over Abyei will remain unresolved despite the Arbitration Court's decision. In what is supposed to be a final decision, the region is to vote on whether it belongs to Sudan or South Sudan in early 2011, on the same day that South Sudan votes on its independence from Sudan. Fears persist that regardless of the vote, fighting will again erupt in Abyei.

"The intention of the [Sudan] president's office was to chase people away," Paguot says of that May 2008 attack, and to replace the Dinka tribe, who are staunchly aligned with the south, with the Messeriya tribe, whom he says Sudan has been arming. Now, "even the Messeriya say they have a place in Abyei," Paguot complains. The peace agreement that ended the fighting calls for Abyei to be controlled by military units composed of soldiers from the north and south, but Paguot says no one knows who truly controls the area. "The commanders are confusing the soldiers" by giving them conflicting orders.

While the Messeriya and the Dinka may be at odds, they share resentment and distrust of the Sudan government led by President al-Bashir. The oil fields in the Abyei region have benefited none in the region with either jobs or revenues. "People working there are not of the Abyei community," Paguot says.

A couple of months before my visit, the oil fields north of Abyei were attacked by local Messeriya tribesmen who claimed to be part of the Justice and Equality Movement (JEM), the largest and probably the best organized of the Darfur rebel groups. The oil field attacks were a bizarre confluence of the fighting in Darfur and the fighting over the oil fields in Abyei. The attack came not long after the Sudanese government's October 2008 announcement of a $260 million deal with the Chinese to expand Sudan's oil operations. The rebels captured nine hostages from an Abyei area oil rig. Reports said five died, two were taken hostage, and two others escaped. Although the kidnappers claimed to be part of JEM, which had boldly attacked Khartoum months earlier, they were in fact Messeriya tribesmen. Upset at the Sudan government's refusal to share the oil wealth, the kidnappers' leader, Abu Humaid Ahmed Dannay, demanded that the Chinese leave and quit developing Sudan's oil. "We don't have any material demands. We want Chinese companies to leave the region immediately because they work with the government," he told a reporter.[2] The Chinese were blamed for ignoring local communities and ruining the environment. Ultimately, the two missing oil workers were found, though one had died.

"The interest of the [Sudan] presidency is the oil," Paguot tells me, echoing the resentment that had flared in the attack on the Chinese oil rigs. "Abyei oil [revenue] is going directly to Khartoum. The president's office is benefiting, but [revenues] are not for the benefit of the community." Two percent of the oil revenues are supposed to flow to Abyei, he says, but no one has seen the money.

While some Messeriya oppose Chinese oil development, they're more concerned about securing grass and water for their cattle, Paguot says, and the Sudanese government is using the Messeriya to drive the Dinka from Abyei. But Messeriya loyalty to Sudan can't be taken for granted. "The people who fought in Abyei were Messeriya," but it was as much for their self-protection as it was against the Dinka. "The Messeriya are protecting their property" first and foremost, he says. Although a tenuous calm has settled over Abyei, Paguot fully expects another flare-up. "They're trying to find a way to make an action," he says of the Sudanese army.

A Chief Speaks

Boing Achuil Bulabec, sixty-five, is a Dinka clan leader who was among the thousands who fled Abyei. He now lives in a walled compound abutting one of the main roads through Agok. We settle into plastic chairs in the shade of a towering mango tree. The attack on Abyei was sudden and ferocious, Bulabec says. People fled. Families were scattered and men, women, and children died. Not only was his house and family attacked, but his cows were taken as well. His friends and relatives "ran away and we don't know what happened to them. If you go, you can see [the destruction] for yourself," he says. "Can you imagine that the government you trust can turn against you and destroy everything you have?" It was a calculated attack and the reason was clear. "What the government needs is to chase the people away . . . and put the Messeriya in, and take advantage of the oil."

Living with the Messeriya has been generally peaceful, Bulabec says. But now the Messeriya carry automatic weapons while tending their cattle. "Tension has increased," creating a serious and dangerous break with the past. During the dry season, the Messeriya land dries, so they migrate from the north to the wetlands surrounding Abyei. When the dry season ends, they return north. But now they're armed and staying. "What [can] you say" when confronted by several armed men demanding water and grass for their cows? he asks.

The Dinka of Abyei are angry and want to be reimbursed for what has been destroyed. "We want total compensation and then we will talk about what will happen to the Messeriya," Bulabec says gravely. "The hope for peace is very small."

Bulabec shrugs when I ask about the oil in Abyei. "Oil is the main point for the government." The government is arming the Messeriya, who see the situation as an opportunity to claim land for their cattle. "They've combined the issues," he says of Sudan. "The Messeriya [are] the front, and the government is behind [them]." With the Messeriya now armed, "they are threatening" even though "they have land and water already." Bulabec fears that the Dinka soon will be driven farther south and will be unable to resist. "What can we do? The [Sudanese] government was to protect us, but there is no protection."

Bulabec wants the international community, in particular the United States, to get more involved, because an outside force is needed to ensure peace. "We will negotiate a peace and we will fight again." The bad blood between the Dinka and the Messeriya cannot be easily forgotten. "How would you feel about someone who took something from you and then comes back and kills you? We are very angry about it. There is nothing. Our houses are burned down."

Merchants of Darfur

While Abyei and South Sudan may be geographically removed from war-ravaged western Darfur, the two regions are inextricably linked. The ties among the people in both regions become obvious as I walk down the main road of Agok, where dozens of merchants from Darfur sit in the shade of their makeshift shops.

Ibrahim Ahmed Gibar came from Kotum in north Darfur. He fled when his community was bombed and overrun by the Sudanese military and *janjaweed* militia in 2004. More than a hundred villagers were killed, he says. "We're not happy with the government." Dressed in a flowing white cotton robe and an embroidered white cap, he explains that friends helped him start a small business, and he goes wherever he can to make money. He looks disgusted when I ask why the Sudanese government is fighting in Darfur. "To destroy all the black people in Darfur," he says flatly. "The same reason they are fighting in Abyei."

This view is shared by Gibar's friend, Mohammed Edriss Abdalla, twenty-eight, who sits nearby on a deeply padded bench. "I don't see a solution other than bringing in the international community," Abdalla says about Abyei. "It needs the presence of the international community." But such action would have to be more aggressive than what the

United Nations and the African Union are doing in Darfur, which he describes as "writing reports every day with nothing happening as a result. People are still suffering." Does he want to return to Darfur? "If there is security," he says, "but with this situation [as it is], we cannot."

Across the road, Omdah Musa Bukor sits amid racks of clothing in his carpet-strewn shop. An ethnic Zaghawa from Darfur, he lost a hundred cows when the *janjaweed* burned his village in 2007. "The *janjaweed* used to loot." His mother is in a refugee camp in Chad and his wife and two sons are in a camp in El Fasher, Darfur. He periodically returns to Darfur, but the government doesn't "want people to live there," he says. "They want land to be there for the Arabs and to use for cattle."

How did he end up in Abyei?

"I heard that Abyei is a good place to start a business," he replies, but the fighting in Abyei has given him second thoughts. "I am not a politician but a businessman. I see the Messeriya and they need the land. It's the same as Darfur. In Darfur, [the government] needs the *janjaweed* . . . and the Messeriya in Abyei. The small Arab [population] is trying to move all the [African] tribes. If the black people take over power, [Arabs] will not be allowed to do anything." Sudan's quest for oil is creating violence throughout the country, he says, especially in Abyei. "If oil is found today, they will come and say 'it is ours,'" he says of the government. Prospects for peace in Sudan are slim without a change in leadership. "There is no solution until al-Bashir is gone. He is only lying to people. There is no peace."

The Battle of Abyei

A fine dust drifts inside the Rested Heart restaurant not far from the merchants' shops on the main road in Agok. Trucks, cars, and donkey-drawn carts rattle on the road outside, and flies buzz over plates of goat stew, beans, and fresh bread. Dau Nyok Chan, twenty-six, a former resident of the town of Abyei, some twenty miles to the north, is telling me about the day he ran for his life. "I was in my house. I heard the sound of guns. People were just running. My sister came and said, 'we are going.'"

Chan zigzagged to dodge bullets and land mines. "It was very dangerous. I ran with only the shirt I was wearing." He paused for a moment in the mayhem to look back. "I saw my house on fire." Then he kept running. "I went into the bush." He found his uncle and spent the next few nights with him, eventually returning home to sift through the ash and rubble. His brother was captured by the notorious Brigade 31 fighters, who had launched the aerial and ground assault on Abyei. "What annoys me is [that] my brother was killed. Soldiers grabbed him [and] cut his throat," he says, dragging a forefinger across his neck. "They know that if a man lives in Abyei, later he will fight with them."

Chan is not alone in his misery. Thousands of others in Abyei suffered similar attacks. Some were burned alive. "People were inside their homes and burned," including the blind and elderly. "Many lost their children" and "still haven't found them."

Sitting with Chan is Nyanlvak Deng Ajup, a bright twenty-four-year-old woman who, like Chan, represents the future of Abyei. Ajup works for a nonprofit aid group doing office work, but she hopes to return to Abyei to resume her studies in computer science. She was in computer class when the May 2008 attack began, she recalls with a shudder. "Suddenly there was fighting. I heard airplanes coming. Then I heard a big bomb [explosion] and ran outside to see what was going on." Ajup was horrified. "Soldiers were fighting in the street," attacking the South Sudan forces that controlled the town. "It was very confusing. Everyone was running away."

Ajup's first impulse was to return home to help her family. But when she arrived, people were fleeing her neighborhood in panic. "There was shooting in the market," Ajup says. She saw a woman and two children who had been shot dead, sprawled on the street. She ran, just like everyone else, and huddled with others through the night in the brush far from town. The next day the fighting quieted, so Ajup ventured back to her home, only to find that it had been burned and looted. "I'm really upset. I went back two times," but it wasn't safe. "I tried to go to stay, but the same army [Brigade 31] is still there."

"It's because of oil and land," Ajup says about the fighting. "They are getting oil, but no one is benefiting. We are just worried for our lives."

Does she see a solution?

Ajup shrugs. "People should sit down and tell [the Sudan government] the oil and land does not belong to them. If they say no, we have to fight." Ajup looks at me with fiery eyes. "The war will never stop until the oil is left to us. I wish I had a gun to fight for my land."

7

A TALE OF TWO SUDANS

I RETURN to Juba from Abyei feeling like I've been to another world, a world unconnected to Juba. But it's not. South Sudan depends almost exclusively on the money it gets from Sudan as part of a revenue-sharing agreement that was included in the 2005 peace agreement with the north. If South Sudan is to have a future, it will be because of the oil and little else.

I am anxious to know what happened at the jungle rendezvous with the Lord's Resistance Army. Is that chapter of Ugandan history, written in blood, finally over? Can the people of northern Uganda and the terrorized regions of northeastern Democratic Republic of the Congo, the Central African Republic, and the western regions of South Sudan finally breathe free? But a stillness hangs over Juba, a depression that is palpable as the delegates to the jungle drift back from Nabanga empty-handed. For the third time, Joseph Kony didn't show. There is a sense now of gathering storm. It will come just weeks later, producing an unimagined outcome. With the journalists back in town once again, I am finally able to deliver my workshop.

I depart Juba a day later, in December 2008, and arrive in the Sudanese capital of Khartoum during the holiday feasting of Eid al-Adha, the Festival of Sacrifice celebrating Abraham's willingness to slay his son Isaac. Again, I am to meet with journalists, but this time from Darfur, Sudan's western province, to discuss the intrica-

cies of the ICC, as I just did in Juba. My entry into Sudan is facilitated by a man whose expertise is obtaining visas for people like
me and clearing a path through customs. There are strict laws and
restrictions on visas into Sudan, I am told, but for a price anything
is possible.

Khartoum is quiet and my downtown hotel largely empty, as most
foreigners have left, knowing nothing gets done during such holidays.
I have several days to fill before meeting with the Darfur journalists, so
I contact Sudanese journalist Ahmed el-Sheikh, who at the time works
for one of Khartoum's dozen or so daily newspapers. He agrees to
arrange meetings for me, the first with Fatihi Halil, a ranking member
of the ruling National Congress Party (NCP) and head of the Sudan
Lawyers Union.

Such encounters are difficult during the day at Eid al-Adha,
because people are visiting family and friends, talking and sharing
lavish feasts. But I am lucky; Halil wants to take the time to make his
point for an international audience.

The lawyers union is particularly influential in Sudanese politics
and society, and Halil does not disappoint my search for insight into
the NCP's worldview.

We are all but the only people in the lavish quarters of the lawyers
union. We sip tall glasses of freshly squeezed, chilled mango juice as
we talk. A tall and imposing man, Halil wears a large white turban and
finely pressed cotton robes. He rails against the ICC and its meddling
in the Darfur conflict.

"Sudan is not a party to the ICC," he complains, and therefore the
ICC has no business getting involved in Sudan and Darfur. "You can't
make a Sudanese citizen [appear] before the ICC." The court has juris-
diction only over the citizens of the countries that are parties to the
agreement that created the court, and neither Sudan nor the United
States are among them. The only way a Sudanese can be brought before
the ICC is by a UN Security Council referral. But even if the Security
Council did that, the referral would be meaningless since the Security
Council "is a political organ."

When I balk, Halil shakes his head.

"If [that] is not the case, the Security Council can refer a US citizen to the ICC." Because the United States is a permanent member of the council and has veto power over any council actions, the council could never order the ICC to investigate a US citizen for war crimes, Halil says.

Sudan does not have the same privilege, he complains, and this proves that "the veto is political." The United States can protect its citizens from the ICC prosecutors, but Sudan can't. It's unfair. Sudan is entitled to similar protections and exemptions. The counterargument, which I don't bring up, is that because the United States is the world's hyperpower and is involved in military actions around the globe, it is uniquely vulnerable to manipulation by the ICC. The argument is flimsy, of course, since the US military justifies much of what it does as defensive acts in the war on terror.

ICC indictments of US officials have been discussed quietly, of course, in the context of Iraq's many combat-related civilian deaths. Some suggest that the killing of noncombatants amounts to a crime of war. The human rights group Iraq Body Count, whose figures are based on news media reports and records from hospitals, morgues, and civil society groups, puts the overall civilian death toll since the US invasion in 2003 at between 94,939 and 103,588.[1] The figure is higher than what has been acknowledged by the Iraqi government. Some have argued that the United States should be held accountable, and the UN Security Council should order the ICC to investigate.

Halil insists that Sudan is suppressing an insurgency in Darfur, not conducting a genocide, contrary to what the US Congress, and more recently the ICC, have charged. "This is an injustice, of course," he tells me. "We must talk about justice and not policies. We are not protecting our citizens who have committed crimes. As a lawyer, I declare we have to have justice. We as lawyers are to defend the rule of law."

The ICC indictment of Sudanese president al-Bashir is undermining the legitimacy of the court, Halil argues, because al-Bashir has been falsely charged. "It must [be] credible," he says of the court. Despite his complaints, Halil ironically says he supports the court. "We back the idea of the ICC. We are behind justice. [But] when a court becomes a political instrument, it becomes unfair."

The Sudanese judiciary can properly prosecute the country's criminals, Halil says. "Our judicial system is competent. Our history of judicial system is well established. It is independent."

News reports swirled at the time that French president Nicolas Sarkozy might try to have the ICC drop its indictment of al-Bashir, but only if Sudan admitted that its actions in Darfur were criminal and agreed to host UN troops. Halil shakes his finger, saying the French have their own humanitarian problems to face. He mentions a French adoption agency's attempt to take about one hundred children out of Chad, claiming they were Darfur refugees. When most of the children were found to have Chadian parents, the group's leaders were jailed but later released. The French don't have a history of humanitarian acts in Algeria, either. "He is not a man who can talk about war crimes and genocide," Halil says of Sarkozy.

The assertion that the fighting in Darfur amounts to a genocide is a political subterfuge meant to undermine Sudan, Halil claims. "When [Moreno-Ocampo] talks of genocide, he is speaking politics. We know who is behind him."

Who is it?

"The Jews are against Sudan," Halil says venomously. All global organizations working for a solution to Darfur, particularly the Save Darfur Coalition, "are Jewish organizations," he says.

At the time, the Save Darfur Coalition is headed by Jerry Fowler, who came to the organization via the US Holocaust Memorial Museum's Committee on Conscience. Save Darfur evolved out of a student action group initially called Students Take Action Now: Darfur (STAND), which began as an outreach activity of the Holocaust Memorial Museum. Save Darfur and similar movements to end the war in Darfur have drawn criticism from other corners as well. In his book *Saviors and Survivors: Darfur, Politics, and the War on Terror,* author Mahmood Mamdani, a professor in the School of International and Public Affairs at Columbia University in New York, complained about the coalition and its Darfur campaign. Despite the debates that swirl over the realities in Darfur, Save Darfur became a cause célèbre, and Mamdani hammers it for becoming a victim of its own success. "That the campaign corresponded less and less to facts on the ground, getting more and more divorced from reality, seemed to make no difference to its credibility. As this happened, Save Darfur increasingly became a feature—and an outstanding one—of the contemporary American political scene," Mamdani wrote.[2] "For the Save Darfur Coalition, advocacy had turned into a series of advertisements. The Campaign is organized by a full-time ad agency. The more the advocacy turned into a sales pitch, the less the ads corresponded to the reality on the ground. Yet, the mobilization continued with increasing success. Save Darfur seemed to have no reality check, either from its board or from the consumer of its product."[3]

Halil does not stop his rant with the ICC indictments or Save Darfur, charging that Jews were behind the embargo on Iraqi oil, and when that failed to topple the government, they "launched the war against Iraq."

I counter that the war on Iraq was endorsed by the UN.

"The Security Council can commit mistakes," he replies.

Halil's complaint that Sudan does not have the same veto power in the UN as the United States or other major powers adroitly avoids answering the charge of genocide and fails to explain why the Sudanese should not be investigated for atrocities in Darfur. Raising the ethno-religious argument that groups like Save Darfur Coalition are "Jewish" only diverts attention from the fact that Save Darfur is saving Muslim lives in Darfur and Chad.

So why are so many people dying and being chased out of Darfur?

"What happened in Darfur cannot be described as a genocide," Halil says. It is a tribal conflict being exploited by outsiders. "This began by some rebels who were backed by some Western circles." This forced Sudan to defend itself. "Any government has to face rebels." France lets one of Darfur's top rebel leaders, Abdel Wahid al-Nur, head of the Sudan Liberation Army, live there in exile. "He [Sarkozy] is protecting terrorists," Halil says.

How do you explain the Darfur villages destroyed by aerial bombardment and militia attacks that reduced them to ash and rubble? I ask. These are attacks on civilians, not rebels, and go far beyond crushing a rebellion.

Halil dismisses my question with a wave. "This is war," he says. "He who began the war is most responsible."

The Curse of Oil

Mahjoub Mohamed Salih is the eighty-one-year-old editor of Khartoum's premiere independent newspaper, *Al-Ayam*, or "The Day." He has been a journalist since 1953 and has seen governments come and go. If nothing else, he's a survivor, and through it all he has become one of Sudan's most esteemed and independent voices. His newspaper has been targeted by the al-Bashir regime and, like other independent and antigovernment news media, was visited nightly by government censors who routinely ripped stories off the pages prior to publication and often confiscated entire press runs as part of the regime's crusade to silence criticism. Salih takes the long view of his newspaper's contemporary troubles and is quietly confident that he and his newspaper will be around after the al-Bashir regime is gone.

"There were [prior] occasions when the government tried to step in" to control the news media, Salih says. One was after South Sudan's late leader, John Garang, died in a helicopter crash in 2005, shortly after the peace deal was signed that ended the country's twenty-three-year civil war. Thousands of Garang supporters rioted in the streets of Khartoum, convinced the government had assassinated him. Martial law was imposed. An international inquiry later said that the helicopter, which belonged to Ugandan president Yoweri Museveni, a close friend of Garang's, had accidentally crashed into a mountainside during a violent rainstorm.

The current wave of censorship came after accusations that the al-Bashir regime supported rebels in neighboring Chad who had attacked the Chadian capital of N'Djamena in February 2008. Chad's president, Idriss Déby, likewise was accused of supporting and providing refuge to Darfur rebels who were fighting the Sudanese government. When the Sudanese press jumped on the issue, the government struck back by imposing crippling censorship, still in place nine months later.

Salih is angry. "A decision to impose 100 percent censorship was not justified," he says in his flawless English. "Nobody wants to ignite more fires." Despite the constitutional protections of the press against government censorship, al-Bashir claims the right to suspend the law when and where he sees fit. Censorship reflects the Sudanese leader's ability to conduct conflicting policies simultaneously. "Sudan is in a unique position to wage war and peace at the same time." Peace is being waged in South Sudan under the 2005 peace agreement, while war is being fought in Darfur. The war in Darfur has also exposed the government's weaknesses, since Darfur rebels boldly attacked Khartoum in May 2008, just six months earlier. "The war [in Darfur] has been very tragic," he says. "It can't go on as it has for six years."

Despite his opposition to the war, Salih says Darfur is misunderstood. "The international community and media are oversimplifying a very complex situation," he says, by "focusing only on the latest stages of the conflict." Darfur is "not an ethnic conflict" because there is very little ethnic difference between the combatants.

Darfur was the last region to be incorporated into Sudan after the fall of British colonial rule. Darfur had long been an independent sultanate that showed its loyalty to Khartoum by way of an annual tribute. But lately Darfur has struggled. "From the start they were handicapped. Darfur is a tribal community," Salih says, and the basis of the conflict pits nomadic pastoralists against farmers over dwindling resources. Al-Bashir's administration made the mistake of "taking sides" in the conflict, he says.

An underlying problem has been a fourfold population increase over the past fifty years. The 1956 census put the population of Sudan at ten million, but it has grown to over forty million. Additionally, the growing deserts in north Darfur have pushed nomadic herdsmen farther south.

Fighting between Chad and Libya to the north, and Chad and the Central African Republic to the south, brought "highly lethal modern arms" into the region. The result: "more people, less land, and lots of armament," Salih says. Instead of negotiating a solution, the government mobilized northern tribesmen. The conflicts in Darfur and South Sudan merged in the 1980s when Sudan used northern tribes to fight in the south, prompting Darfur rebels to ally with South Sudan against the Khartoum government.

Even as the war in Darfur is winding down at the end of 2008, Salih predicts that the lingering resentments from the two to three hundred thousand dead and the two million displaced, most of whom are still in Chad, will lead to more fighting. "If the land problem is solved without employment and development, in a few years' time the conflict will erupt again."

As in Darfur, the fighting in South Sudan is over resources, Salih explains. In 1972, Abyei was part of the north, and no one objected, "because there was nothing to fight about. The discovery of oil brought about [today's] conflict. We are witnessing the curse of oil," because the north and South Sudan both depend on it. "In both cases, they need the oil. There is tension and it is serious and we don't know how it will turn out."

The decision by the Permanent Court of Arbitration in The Hague to divide the Abyei oil region between the north and south may not be a lasting solution, Salih says, despite the fact that both parties have agreed to abide by it. "I am hoping that both sides will decide [it] is too small a problem to go back to war."

Though the vote for independence and the future of Abyei is looming in the south, Salih is skeptical that it will solve much. "Separation [from Sudan] is not going to solve the problem of war and peace," he says, pointing to the long war between Ethiopia and Eritrea that eventually led to Eritrean independence.

I tell him about the new army tanks I saw at military posts in South Sudan just days earlier, and about the reports that arms shipments were headed toward the south. Salih nods. The north-south 2005 peace agreement allowed both sides to arm themselves. "If they have an army, it is only natural that they arm."

Oil's effect on Sudan is felt in ways that few imagine, Salih suggests, due to the precipitous drop in the price of oil from over $100 per barrel down to about $45 per barrel. "All sides will have to face the fact that the situation will be affected negatively by the price of oil." Falling oil prices devastate the Sudan economy and make the control of oil even more critical. Since about two-thirds of the Sudanese budget is based on oil, Sudan considered new tax increases on imported cars and mobile telephone services at the time. Oil prices are even more critical to South Sudan, which derives 97 percent of its budget from the fifty-fifty oil revenue sharing agreement with Khartoum.

Salih is troubled by the ICC's pursuit of justice in Darfur. "There is no peace without justice," Salih agrees, "but it is equally true that you can't have justice without peace." In resolving Darfur, peacemakers need to think about the big picture. "There are lots of things in addition to justice" that have to be accomplished, he says. "Do you want to stop the conflict, or to ignite the conflict? I think it is going to complicate the situation there if you go ahead with it," he says of the ICC's indictment of al-Bashir.

A similar case has been made regarding the twenty-year war in northern Uganda with the rebel Lord's Resistance Army. In effect, the argument is that an international indictment only corners the accused and prevents a peaceful resolution of the fighting. In reality, this argument is just an excuse not to prosecute those responsible for terrible war crimes, I say. Letting accused war criminals off the hook under the threat of more war is not rational.

"I would like to see those who committed crimes see justice, but [what] if it means more war?" Salih asks. "If we don't have peace, we are going to jail two or three people but at a high price." ICC prosecution "is a detriment to peace."

Murtada al-Ghali

It is a warm and sunny day when el-Sheikh and I take a taxi over the Nile to Khartoum's sister city of Omdurman. Both cities seem to be asleep. Stores are closed, save for an occasional corner grocery or small restaurant. Few cars are on the road. We find Murtada al-Ghali, editor of the Khartoum-based newspaper *Ajras al-Huriya*, which means "Freedom Bells," relaxing inside his spacious house on a side street in Omdurman. He greets us, then excuses himself to say good-bye to friends. Like Halil, Murtada is a tall man, and as we settled into cushioned chairs, he adjusts a large white turban.

Al-Ghali also struggles under the government's severe censorship, since his publication is viewed as hostile. "They are targeting newspapers to harm them financially by banning advertisements." Freedom Bells is considered an opposition newspaper because it is funded by the South Sudanese. The censorship is unnecessary, al-Ghali says, because South Sudan's dominant political party, the Sudanese People's Liberation Movement, is virtually powerless against Sudan's controlling National Congress Party (NCP) in Sudan's unity government. "They [the NCP] have the tools of the state in their hands, and the money," he says.

Al-Ghali dismisses my comment that support from South Sudan creates a bias, even if it is only perceived. He uses writers from all corners of Sudan. "They are lacking a forum," he says of the south, and want their views made public, which is why they support al-Ghali's newspaper. "We want southerners to speak out." He supports the 2005 peace agreement between the north and south and a democratic transition for South Sudan, but insists that "this [newspaper] is run by the journalists only. We are not writing for the opposition. We are a newspaper run for all parties. We have diversity among our editors."

He says that the results of the 2010 national election, which is currently approaching, will be dubious, because two million voters in Darfur who would likely cast ballots against al-Bashir and other government-backed candidates have been forced out of the country.

A census to be taken prior to a vote clearly will not reflect the true population of Darfur. "How can it be a free and fair election?" he asks. "We have many, many problems."

Despite the glaring electoral deficiencies, al-Ghali thinks the election has to proceed, saying, "A bad election is better than no election. It might give them legitimacy," he says, and it might remove the government's dependence on force to impose its will. (The election will, in fact, reaffirm al-Bashir as president and have the effect that al-Ghali predicts, which is a marked decrease in the Darfur conflict.)

The violence around Abyei is over oil, al-Ghali agrees, though conflict between the Messeriya and the Dinka has been documented since British colonial times. It's unclear if the Messeriya are truly behind the fighting, although the Khartoum government's involvement is widely rumored. "The government used to arm those people to fight the rebels in the south," al-Ghali says, so the current fighting has historical precedent. Even so, the Messeriya are not simply tools of Khartoum but are looking after their own interests. "The Messeriya are trying to take care of themselves."

Darfur casts a pall over everything in Sudan, al-Ghali says. The longer fighting continues, the more ethnic issues are exposed. "The people being harmed are the so-called African Sudanese." Peace can only be achieved if the government listens to the Darfuris' complaints and responds with "assurances that Darfur will be part of the solution."

When people don't trust their government, they turn to their own ethnic group. "People try to give some [ethnic] identity" to the fighting in Darfur, he says, but the conflict is about "ownership of land." What once was common grazing land in Darfur is now being fought over, along with the right to dig water wells. The war in Darfur has multiple causes: drought and scarcity; nomads versus city dwellers; traditionalism versus modernity.

Khartoum has made Darfur much worse than it needs to be, al-Ghali asserts. "They can't control what they have made. Many areas are out of their hands. The whole of Sudan is out of their hands." President al-Bashir has less power than ever. "It has weakened his regime," he

says of the complexities surrounding Darfur. When the ICC indictment is added, the situation becomes unmanageable. "They [the al-
Bashir regime] pretend they don't care about the ICC," al-Ghali says.
But in reality, "they are very sensitive about this issue. I think they do
care." The indictments have generated a growing rift within the ruling
NCP. "Some say there is some sort of split within the NCP over how to
deal with the ICC."

Is the pressure on al-Bashir enough to make him step down?

Al-Ghali shakes his head, saying that too many people have too
much invested in the regime for al-Bashir to resign. The president
is backed by "persons of wealth and power in Sudan," and "all these
people are afraid [that] if al-Bashir disappears from the scene," they
will lose everything. Fear is "the nature of this regime," and it drives
government censorship. "They can't stand independent newspapers,"
which is why his Freedom Bells has been harassed.

Newspapers are widely read in the city, al-Ghali tells me, and
therefore powerful, "more . . . than political powers and individual
trade unions. The news media is the most active [in presenting] the
political agenda to the people of Sudan. They fear [news media]," he
says, "because it is not in their hands."

"We [independent journalists] are people who are looking for a
new Sudan," al-Ghali says. "We are for the unity" that was expressed
in the 2005 peace agreement that also outlined a new constitution for
Sudan. "We are against the abuse of human rights. We are for margin-
alized people. We are very proud about that. We want the right of the
people to know."

Farouk Abu-Eissa

A day later, I meet with Farouk Abu-Eissa, a former foreign minister
for Sudan and leading member of the opposition alliance to the al-
Bashir regime. On the cool, grassy lawn of his suburban Khartoum
home not far from the city's airport, he smiles and says the house has
a secret. It was an al-Qaeda guest house for friends and visitors of

Osama bin Laden when he lived in Sudan. I look around with a shudder as I gratefully accept his offer of freshly squeezed juice.

Abu-Eissa has little hope that the Darfur conflict can be settled by the al-Bashir regime. "Even if the war is stopped, there are problems that need to be faced. The Darfur people have legitimate demands. [But] the government doesn't want to accept that there are legitimate rights there that need to be addressed." The demands of the Darfuris include a return to the "greater Darfur," he explains, which is the unified Darfur that existed before the region was divided into thirds by the Khartoum government. Other demands include equitable division of wealth based on population rather than the current dearth of government services in Darfur.

The Darfuris also want a vice president who can represent them in President al-Bashir's office, in part to ensure that they're compensated for the losses inflicted by the Sudanese military and the *janjaweed*. But so far the government has refused to acknowledge these damages or to provide compensation. Finally, Abu-Eissa says, is the demand to stop the war and release all prisoners and detainees. "It could stop tomorrow, but they [the government] don't want it," he says.

A lasting peace in Darfur will "not be attainable unless a united Khartoum government is ready to go into a democratic transformation." An effective government would have to enforce the rule of law and create a truly independent judiciary, which now is a "partisan judiciary" since almost all of the judiciary members belong to al-Bashir's party. "Unless we do that, we can't maintain peace in the south and solve the Darfur situation." Abu-Eissa predicts that the country unfortunately "will continue" along the "narrow Islamic movement" path al-Bashir follows.

Rather than calling the war a genocide, Abu-Eissa prefers the term "ethnic cleansing." While the distinctions are vague, he says that the quest for oil and minerals is what's truly behind the conflict. "This policy was ethnic cleansing after oil was discovered" in north Darfur, which he says also has water, oil, and uranium. "That is the true reason for the struggle: wealth."

Most people call the war in Darfur an ethnic or tribal conflict, I say.

That's an "old reason," he replies. "It is not the problem as they say it is." With control of the water sources, those in power can begin raising cattle, and "they can make lots of money." The same holds true with control of the land in northern Darfur, said to have oil and other minerals.

Though at the time I doubt Abu-Eissa's suggestion that minerals are behind the fighting in Darfur, in early 2010 the Sudanese government will announce that oil development rights are being awarded in Darfur. At about the same time, Sudan's oil minister will say an oil field in South Darfur province will also be offered to investors.

The North Darfur oil is to be developed jointly by a company known as the Greater Sahara group, Sudan's state-run oil company Sudapet Co., and a company called AlQahtani, according to Sudanese Petroleum Corporation's website.[4]

It's perhaps a risky move, considering that the war in Darfur is far from over. Ahmed Hussein, a spokesman for the Justice and Equality Movement rebel group in Darfur, will immediately announce that only "after peace is reached, can companies invest in Darfur's oil. The government uses the money from oil investment against the people, not for them."[5]

With oil development in the offing, the loss of up to three hundred thousand lives and the displacement of two million people in Darfur come into focus. Even as the 2005 peace agreement with South Sudan was being hammered out, al-Bashir's government in Khartoum was ramping up the war in Darfur. Perhaps the regime had seen the writing on the wall. Perhaps they knew that the south would eventually be lost as the international community ensured that South Sudan's independence vote would take place in 2011 as negotiated. The loss of the south, along with its oil, meant Khartoum had to look elsewhere for wealth. Elsewhere was Darfur.

8

ARMIES AND
EXPLOITATION

L ESS THAN a week after my departure from Khartoum, in December 2008, the Ugandan army attacks the camps of Joseph Kony's Lord's Resistance Army deep in the heart of the Congo's Garamba National Forest. The attack ripples through the international community, which has coddled Kony and kept him alive on the premise that he will come to his senses and sign a peace deal. But that is not to be. Soon it becomes known that the United States was behind the attack, having provided the Ugandans with military advisers and trainers and a reported $1 million in fuel and supplies.

But Kony escaped. According to witnesses, Kony learned of the strike and fled with most of his army of ruthless former child soldiers, splitting it into three groups. One group moved north toward the Central African Republic, a second moved west, deeper into the Congo, and a third pushed to the southeast. Each went on a three-week-long killing spree that claimed nearly a thousand innocent lives. It was classic LRA. Strike the softest and most vulnerable of targets: defenseless men, women, and children of the Congo who have nothing to do with the LRA or its so-called rebellion against the Ugandan government.

Details of Uganda's botched attack emerge along with speculation that Kony was tipped off. The attack was supposed to take place at dawn, but the camp was apparently shrouded in fog at that hour, so the air assault was delayed until nearly noon, when the mist lifted. The only ones in the camp to see the bombs drop were the abducted women and children that Kony left behind. Kony's soldiers were only hours from the camp, and they might have been attacked by ground forces if the Ugandan army had been in place. But the Ugandan force didn't arrive at Kony's camp for two days. When the soldiers walked into the LRA camp, all they found was a few laptop computers, radios, and phones. The camp was empty of humanity.

Two years later, Kony will still be on the loose and killing.

Anatomy of Chaos

In early 2009, reports of the LRA's vicious attacks on villagers continued, and condemnations rained in from around the world. But Kony and his army remained a sideshow to the carnage that gripped eastern Congo. As I was preparing for my trip to Sudan in late 2008, Congolese militia commander Laurent Nkunda had led his Tutsi CNDP militia on a blitzkrieg that drove the ragtag Congolese army out of the mineral-rich Masisi region and sent the soldiers scrambling through the befuddled ranks of the UN peacekeepers. Nkunda stopped at the outskirts of Goma, but only after 250,000 civilians had been uprooted, driving the total number of displaced persons to nearly two million. Nkunda gloated and, in a pique of self-delusion, threatened to topple Congo's President Joseph Kabila—suggesting a repeat of what the Rwandans and Ugandans had done to Congolese dictator Mobutu some twelve years earlier.

But the game in eastern Congo suddenly changed in late January 2009, when the seemingly untouchable Nkunda was taken into custody by the Rwandan government and held incommunicado, a bizarre turn of events that puzzled many. But over the next few months, the reasons became clear. Nkunda's arrest was the opening move in a dark and deadly game pitting helpless pawns against greedy power brokers.

Shortly after Nkunda's arrest, the Rwandan army crossed into eastern Congo, leading a joint operation with the Congolese national forces aimed at driving the Hutu FDLR militia out of North and South Kivu. The chaotic and hapless Congolese army could never defeat Nkunda's disciplined fighters, nor could it do much about the Hutu FDLR, who happily plundered the region's minerals like everyone else. In addition, elements of the Congolese army worked closely with the Hutu militias, a relationship that stretched back to the waning days of the Mobutu regime in the mid-1990s. It became apparent also that Rwandan president Paul Kagame had bowed to international pressure and agreed to sideline Nkunda in a peacemaking gesture. But the stipulation was that an alternative force would be created to counter the strength of the Hutu FDLR. The Congo's President Kabila had little choice but to agree. It was a big gamble, but one that might quell the endless violence roiling through the eastern provinces.

The Congolese-Rwandan operation was called Umoja Wetu, which means "our unity," and was surprisingly brief, ending in late February 2009, when the Rwandan army went home claiming to have killed hundreds of Hutus. The military sweep was a token gesture at best. The Hutu militia was still there, said to number nearly 4,500 fighters, and everyone knew it. The most vocal cynics said that the operation was never about the Hutus but was designed so that the Tutsis could reclaim mines that had been lost to the Hutus. In a November 2009 report, the UN Group of Experts monitoring the region revealed the dismal reality of the joint operation:

> The effectiveness of Umoja Wetu was diminished by the limited resources and logistical capacities of [the Congolese army]. It appears that the operations were further crippled owing to the embezzlement of several million United States dollars in operational funds by top officers in [the Congolese army] and [the Rwandan army]. While the Group could not document this misappropriation of funds, it received consistent reports both from presidential sources in Kinshasa and from [Congo-

lese army] officials involved in the operations. During Umoja Wetu the Group also received consistent reports that [the Rwandan army] and newly integrated [Tutsi militia soldiers] working in tandem had cleared several areas of civilian populations, particularly in [the] Walikale [district of the North Kivu], where newly integrated former [Tutsi militia] troops planted the seeds of their present control over principle axes in mining-rich zones of the territory.[1]

Since the Hutu FDLR forces simply returned to their original positions when the Congolese-Rwandan forces withdrew, a second military operation called Kimia II was undertaken with the support of the UN peacekeepers. But the UN peacekeepers were criticized when elements of the Congolese army they supported began to loot and rape.

Though this was never publicly stated, the Kagame-Kabila agreement amounted to a bleak admission of the absolute failure of the Congolese government, which has little command or control over eastern Congo or its own army of drunken thugs. The soldiers are barely trained, if at all, and are rarely paid, which leaves most of them to take advantage of their status as government troops. This did not escape the attention of UN experts, who summed up the problem in May 2009: "Delays in the disbursement of [national army] salaries have also exacerbated indiscipline within the newly integrated [army] units . . . resulting in ongoing human rights violations perpetrated by [the national army], including looting and attacks on the civilian population."[2]

Soon, yet another permutation of the agreement came to light. The second sweep was conducted by the same ethnic Tutsis who had been chasing the Hutu rebels all along. Nothing had changed since the years following the 1994 genocide, only that now the ethnic battle had been institutionalized.

After his arrest, Nkunda was replaced as head of the Tutsi CNDP by his top commander, Bosco Ntaganda, the man indicted by the ICC.

Ntaganda was effectively leading the second military operation against the Hutu FDLR militia in eastern Congo, but as an officer in the newly expanded Congolese army in the eastern provinces, the bulk of which were Tutsi fighters of Nkunda's CNDP militia.

Incorporating former combatants into the Congolese army had a loopy logic. One supposed these former enemies wouldn't kill one another. Though a shallow gesture at creating peace, it had good propaganda value for the Congolese officials who stood to benefit by letting the Tutsis keep their slice of the region's mineral wealth. With the former combatants under one command, the government could claim that its army was "in control," though of course it was not in control and never had been.

By May 2009, the Congolese announced that twelve thousand new soldiers had joined the national army, half of whom were the former CNDP led by Ntaganda. Another 2,800 were the Hutu-aligned PARECO militia, whose leader I spoke with in chapter 4. Another 3,200 soldiers came from the disparate Mai-Mai militias.[3]

But even as these new forces were being integrated into the national army, cracks in the facade began to open. Few soldiers turned in their weapons. The twelve thousand soldiers gave up only about 3,500 weapons, and most of them came from the Tutsi CNDP. Only 680 came from the PARECO fighters.[4] Furthermore, UN experts reported that significant stockpiles of weapons remained under the personal control of the former CNDP commanders now in the national army. If the integration of the army failed, those stockpiles of weapons would allow the Tutsi militia to regroup and quickly rearm.

Additional problems surfaced. By April 2009, UN experts found that the ranks of the national army were already dwindling. Desertions had become rife, many from former CNDP units, who apparently didn't want to be part of the national forces, and some from the former PARECO units. But the fighters weren't going home. They were joining smaller militias and the Hutu FDLR. Deserters from the Mai-Mai militias were going back to their old units. By the middle of 2009, it seemed the new national army was disintegrating, and each of its constituents was claiming the same territory it had controlled before joining the national army.

The logic then became clear. Integration of former combatants could work, of course, only if the same fighters could continue to profit from the mines they controled. The units and their commanders knew that the government wasn't going to pay the soldiers, so they relied on income from the mines. Now in Congolese uniforms and still led by Ntaganda, the former Tutsi CNDP fighters once again controlled Masisi. They began collecting taxes to the tune of about $250,000 a month. They even issued CNDP-stamped receipts to those who paid the army's tax.[5] These taxpayers were the miners hauling gold, tin, and coltan out of the mountains and into Goma.

The biggest prize in North Kivu is the Bisie mine. By far the largest producer of quality tin ore (cassiterite) in the region, the Bisie mine is a rust-colored, deeply scarred, and heavily punctured mound in the middle of the jungle. Its pits, tunnels, and caves are worked by many hundreds of miners, mostly local villagers, and scores of others attracted by the promise of riches. The miners work in miserable conditions, hacking at the rock and soil with sticks, picks, and shovels, dragging the ore in buckets and by ropes, and selling it to local middlemen, buyers called *négociants.*

When UN experts visited the mine in early 2009, they found a bizarre division of control. Congolese army officers were extorting money from anyone they encountered, from the miners to the buyers who are vaguely described as working with "various mineral-exporting companies." The army wasn't there by accident, either; Kinshasa officials had sent them. But the army didn't control everything. Part of the mine was in the grip of a former Tutsi CNDP commander who had been integrated into the national army. When government mining agents arrived, saying they were going to inspect the mine, he sent them packing. The UN described the situation this way:

Part of the mine is under the control of some senior [army] officers appointed by Kinshasa before January 2009, but it has also now been partially occupied by elements taking orders from an ex-CNDP commander, now part of the [national army], which has expelled Government mining agents from the mining site. The mine was controlled by elements of the [army's] 85th Brigade until earlier in 2009, when the Government persuaded the commander of the 85th Brigade to vacate the site.[6]

In yet another corner of North Kivu, far from the Bisie mine, the UN found other former CNDP affiliates still in control of a critical revenue source for the region—the Uganda border crossing at Bunagana, the place where I had gotten my first taste of eastern Congo in 2006. UN experts estimated that in 2009, about $200,000 a month was being "lost" there by the Congolese government, since the import/export fees were going into the pockets of former CNDP fighters. Congolese customs officials who were sent to Bunagana to take control of the crossing were instead turned away by CNDP partisans loyal to Laurent Nkunda, who was still in Rwandan custody. Not surprisingly, their leader was Nkunda's brother, who controlled much of the money moving through Bunagana. Eventually he was arrested for possession of an illegal arms cache.

Bosco Ntaganda's wife was also a loyalist. She was found importing twenty-six tons of rice and 250 boxes of tomatoes across the Congo-Uganda border, presumably destined for her husband's now-Congolese troops.[7] Commander Ntaganda, meanwhile, remained in the thick of the plunder even as an indictee of the ICC. Complaints about the government's inert attitude toward the accused war criminal were blithely ignored. Like Nkunda, his predecessor as head of the former CNDP, Ntaganda, seemingly beyond reach, quietly collected his mineral taxes.

Nor did the Hutu militias sit still after the two military operations designed to eliminate them. FDLR units counterattacked the reconstituted Congolese forces, recapturing some of their lost mines. The Hutu militias in South Kivu had been largely untouched in any case. They occupied the national parks, which UN experts report are "used by the

FDLR as rear bases where they can also continue exploiting mineral sites out of reach of [the national army]."⁸ The biggest prizes for the Hutus were the glittering gold mines hidden in the forests around the town of Lubero in North Kivu, which the Hutu FDLR had been forced to vacate under the short-lived government attacks early in 2009. UN experts explained the situation this way:

> As at the end of April 2009, [Hutu] FDLR continue to con-
> trol many of the same cassiterite mining sites in South Kivu
> as were identified . . . in 2008, and have regained control of
> important gold mines west of Lubero after initially being dis-
> placed from them during [operation] Kimia II. The Group has
> also obtained information that the FDLR gold trade to [the
> towns of Butembo and Bujumbura] . . . remains active.⁹

The Hutu militias in the Kivus did not act in isolation but were supported by an extensive Hutu diaspora. After a detailed analysis of hundreds of telephone records for numbers belonging to FDLR military commanders, the UN experts found "frequent calls by FDLR military commanders to more than 20 countries in Europe, Africa, and North America."¹⁰

The Hutus apparently were and would continue to be led in absentia by Ignace Murwanashyaka, who fled Rwanda in the mid-1990s to settle in Germany. A reputed *génocidaire*, Murwanashyaka appeared to have been working closely with another Rwandan, Straton Musoni, who also lived in Germany. From this distant position, the two channeled money and supplies flowing out of and into eastern Congo.

Yet another tracked by the UN experts was Jean-Marie Vianney Higiro, who had been living in the United States and was said to lead a Hutu breakaway militia group in the Kivu provinces known as the Rally for Unity and Democracy (RUD). As recently as early 2009, Higiro was a professor at Western New England College in Springfield, Massachusetts, and acknowledged his affiliation with the RUD to the *Washington Post*. The RUD was thought to have retaliated against civilians accused of cooperating with Congolese forces in the early 2009 anti-Hutu sweep. UN experts revealed that after these Hutu fighters returned to claim lost territories, they issued printed warnings against government cooperation, and to underscore their threats, they burned down 250 homes, killing a dozen people.[11]

Minerals and Militias

The two military operations carried out by Congolese forces in 2009 did nothing to bring about a change in eastern Congo, UN experts reported. "[The] FDLR continues to operate in mining sites in South Kivu and has even expanded into new sites in the province since January 2009. . . . [Also,] many of the traders involved in purchasing cassiterite [tin ore], gold and other minerals from FDLR areas in South Kivu in 2008 continue to do so [and] . . . gold-trading networks linked to FDLR in North Kivu . . . remain active."[12]

None of the entities in eastern Congo operate in isolation. The mineral trade is a wide-ranging and somewhat scattered system by which ore flows out of the region and money flows in. The militias that control the mines don't dig the ore themselves, of course. Instead, they control access to the mines and tax the miners, usually local villagers, for access to the mining pits. The taxes are paid in cash or ore, and it's not unusual for the tax to be as much as 20 or 30 percent of the value of the ore or of the ore itself. The miners, and the militias that control the mines, then sell their bags of ore to the *négociants*. The *négociants*, in turn, sell the minerals to buyers and exporters, known as *comptoirs*, in the provincial capitals of Goma and Bukavu.

Activists have long insisted that one way to stop the bloodshed in eastern Congo is to choke off the money supply that allows the militias not only to survive but to thrive. This can best be done if the *comptoirs* refuse to buy ore that comes from the so-called conflict mines controlled by militias and, now, elements of the Congolese army. The trick is knowing the exact source of the ore after it is bagged and hauled to a mineral market where *négociants* come to buy it. The *comptoirs* have long argued that the origin of the ore is not their problem. It is the *négociants* who have that responsibility, since they and not the *comptoirs* are on the ground and in the regions.

While this seems like a plausible argument, UN experts have reported that most *comptoirs* work hand-in-hand with *négociants* and consider them employees. *Comptoirs* often help *négociants* register with the government and provide them with the money to buy the minerals. The UN has concluded that "the . . . *comptoirs* are indeed responsible for the purchase of their minerals."[13]

But the *comptoirs* do not operate alone, either. They sell the ore to mineral traders, who are often freelance buyers for the global mining companies who own the smelters that convert and refine the raw ore into useable metal. Their metal ingots, in turn, are sold to a multitude of companies around the world who make parts and components for hundreds, if not thousands, of products. In their reports from 2008 and 2009, UN experts identified two such companies involved in the minerals trade in the eastern Congo as Traxys and Trademet.[14]

The Traxys website describes the company this way: "Traxys primarily focuses on the marketing and sourcing of base metals and concentrates, minor and alloying metals, industrial minerals and chemicals, materials for steel mills and foundries, and carbon products. Along the way, we manage all parts of the supply chain from producer to consumer—worldwide."[15] Trademet is a Belgium-based company specializing in "ores, primarily tantalite [coltan] and cassiterite [tin]," according to the Minor Metals Trade Association.[16]

When UN experts met with Traxys executives in the company's Brussels offices in March 2009, executives explained that Traxys purchased ore from the same *comptoirs* it had dealt with in the past, but now "were doing so on the basis of waivers signed by those suppliers, who were claiming that their sources of minerals were not controlled by armed groups."[17] When UN experts asked Traxys executives to document the claims, the company in late April 2009 suspended its ore purchases in the Kivus, saying, "There is no acceptable solution to this issue but to stop any purchase of material."[18]

Traxys's action had an immediate effect, particularly on certain *comptoirs* identified in the May 2009 UN report as having purchased ore that came either from Hutu FDLR-controlled mines or from Tutsi CNDP-controlled mines for resale on the world market. Namegabe Mudekereza, the head of Groupe Olive and one of the South Kivu mineral traders named by UN experts, said that in May 2009 he received a letter from Traxys stating that it had stopped all mineral buying in the region. Mudekereza heads the local traders association known as the Enterprise Federation of the Congo. "This will have a very bad impact for our business," he told a reporter, adding that Traxys was one of the major buyers of tin from Congo. UN experts also named the Etablissement Muyeye as a buyer of ore from mines controlled by the FDLR. Byaboshi Muyeye, the head of Etablissement Muyeye, confirmed that he too received a letter from Traxys suspending ore purchases. Both men denied that they deal in ore from FDLR mines.[19]

When Trademet responded to the UN's request for information about how it avoided the purchase of so-called conflict minerals, the company's answers were incomplete or unclear. "Trademet has also replied to a number of questions submitted by the Group, but did not address the Group's query regarding the issue of due diligence. The Group would welcome the publication of due diligence plans by companies named in the Group's last report as well as other consumers of Congolese minerals."[20]

Choking the Money Supply

Who is responsible—or not—for the flow of money that funds the militia conflicts and the resulting humanitarian catastrophe in eastern Congo? In July 2009 the London-based human rights group Global Witness issued a study that amounted to an indictment of the global companies that buy minerals from eastern Congo. Titled *Faced with a Gun, What Can You Do?* and subtitled *War and the Militarization of Mining in Eastern Congo*, the Global Witness report argued that the companies buying ore, and ultimately the companies that use the metals derived from the ores, are responsible for fueling the war in eastern Congo that has left millions dead. The report explained it this way:

> In their broader struggle to seize economic, political and military power, all the main warring parties have carried out the most horrific human rights abuses, including widespread killings of unarmed civilians, rape, torture and looting, recruitment of child soldiers to fight in their ranks, and forced displacement of hundreds of thousands of people. The lure of eastern Congo's mineral riches is one of the factors spurring them on. By the time these minerals reach their ultimate destinations—the international markets in Europe, Asia, North America and elsewhere—their origin, and the suffering caused by this trade, has long been forgotten.[21]

UN experts had been reporting the same information for nearly a decade, and the Global Witness report reinforced their findings. Global Witness urged immediate action: first, cut off militia and Congolese army access to mining sites in eastern Congo and international trade networks; second, end the impunity for those engaged in illicit mineral exploitation and trade by pressuring the Congolese government, its neighbors, and all other countries where these companies are registered; and third, hold all companies trading in minerals from eastern Congo accountable through legal action against trade that fuels the conflict.

The Global Witness report detailed the complex set of players in the minerals trade, and on the ground the most brutal of them all seemed to be the Hutu FDLR militia. In some cases, individual FDLR commanders claimed their own mines in South Kivu, but they also worked with Congolese army commanders. "The . . . supposedly battlefield enemies often act in collaboration, carving up territory and mining areas through mutual agreement and sometimes sharing the spoils. The [Hutus] use roads controlled by the [national army], and vice versa, without difficulty. Minerals produced by the [Hutu militias] are sent out through local airports controlled by the [national army] in South Kivu."[22]

Officials within provincial governments were also involved in smuggling from gold mines at Lubero in North Kivu, some of which were controlled by Hutu rebels. The neighboring countries of Rwanda and Burundi were involved as well, acting as conduits for moving minerals out of the region.

Global Witness identified two companies among those buying eastern Congolese minerals moving into the global market. One was Thailand Smelting and Refining Company Ltd. (Thaisarco), said to be the world's fifth-largest tin producer and owned by the British firm Amalgamated Metal Corporation (AMC). Not long after the Global Witness report went public, Thaisarco suspended purchasing eastern Congolese minerals, citing negative publicity. At the time, ironically, the company had been working to establish a system of identification that might, if followed diligently, identify and eliminate the purchase of minerals said to be funding militant groups.

Global Witness also complained that the foreign governments who regulated companies operating in eastern Congo had turned a blind eye to the bloodshed and chaos in the Kivus by not demanding that these companies be held accountable. The illogic of the situation is that these governments, including the United States, pour aid money into eastern Congo to treat the suffering caused by fighting over minerals—the same minerals that ultimately end up in the hands of global companies and consumers.

Eastern Congo has been an orgy of greed and blood. Money is being made in eastern Congolese minerals, and there's no one to stop those who will do anything to get it. In August 2009, I return to Goma wondering how long this tragedy can continue.

9

WOES OF WALIKALE

"MINERALS ARE not only the source of conflict, they are the source of the persistence of war and conflict," says Thomas Luanda, sitting amid the clutter of his small office in Goma. A lawyer and director of his own nonprofit group, Luanda also is a native of Walikale, one of the richest mineral districts in eastern Congo and home to the lucrative Bisie tin mine. He grew up surrounded by mines and knows firsthand of the conflicts to control them. He smiles at my question about the links between minerals and war. "Before 1993, these minerals were not known," he says of cassiterite (tin), wolferite (tungsten), and coltan (tantalum). "Only gold was of interest." More important, the region was peaceful.

That changed soon after the 1994 Rwandan genocide. Coltan, short for columbite-tantalite, is a colloquial name used in central Africa for ore that contains tantalum and related minerals. (When mixed with other related minerals, tantalum is also called tantalite.) Coltan was little known in the region until the meteoric rise in mobile telephone technology and the widespread use of computers and video gaming devices in about 1996. Coltan is used in electronics because it effectively resists heat and is highly conductive. Tin is in high demand for electronics as well; it has replaced lead as the primary component of solder in electronic devices. Demand for these minerals stoked the flames of war as exploitation grew, launching a dozen years of death in eastern Congo. While the history of war in the region is known, the demand for minerals that coincided with and in part caused the wars has largely been ignored.

When Rwanda and Uganda invaded eastern Congo in 1996 to back the late Laurent-Désiré Kabila and his Alliance of Democratic Forces for the Liberation of Congo-Zaire (AFDL), it was not for purely political reasons, Luanda says.

"The AFDL and Rwanda were involved in the exploitation of minerals." While Kabila's forces marched to Kinshasa, taking it in late May 1997, some Rwandans, Ugandans, and Burundians stayed behind to grab the minerals. "This brought an explosion in the number of *comptoirs*" in North and South Kivu provinces, Luanda continues. When Uganda and Rwanda split from Kabila in 1998 and created their new army, called the Rally for Congolese Democracy (RCD), strong enough to depose Kabila, he turned to Zimbabwe, Namibia, and Angola for allies. With their help, Kabila held onto most of the country, but at a cost of millions of lives.

Back in the Kivu provinces, Kabila turned to his former enemies, the Hutu FDLR militias who had been competing with the Tutsis for control of eastern Congo's mines. Peace talks in July 1999 led to the cessation of fighting, but the Ugandans and Rwandans stayed, giving rise to ethnic militias that fought for control of land and minerals. The Congolese government was helpless. "War cut off the region from Kinshasa," Luanda says. Still today, everyone in eastern Congo is involved in mineral exploitation one way or another. "That's why it's so hard to stop."

It was a perfect storm for plunder. According to Luanda, "no taxes were paid." As mining grew, so did the muscle of the militias. "All rebel groups in the region [were] backed by neighboring countries. They were supported by others outside those countries. [Mining] strengthened the rebels' [ability] to resist the government. It was very good business."

Ethnic hatred was fueled by the growing greed. "The ethnic group that got rich was the Tutsi. They led the military groups."

Of course, "the other ethnic groups became angry," particularly the Hutu FDLR, who worked just as hard as the Tutsis to exploit the mines and minerals. "Some minerals went to [the Rwandan capital of] Kigali by helicopter," he says. "That's how the FDLR [also] became rich."

The Mai-Mai, meanwhile, eastern Congo's homegrown militias, who view both the Hutus and the Tutsis as foreigners, were enraged. "It was their mines," Luanda says of the Mai-Mai. "They banded together to protect their lands."

The result was a profusion of militias wreaking havoc wherever they went, killing any who might counter their control of the mines.

Even today, as the Congolese government tries to exert control, the situation is fragile. "Some politicians are using armed groups for political opposition. Government forces are also involved [in mining]. They don't want to see war end," Luanda explains. It would cut off their source of money. A Kinshasa political figure recently claimed ownership of several mines in the Masisi district despite his absence from the region. The villagers, who mine the property and have endured vicious militias to protect their rights, balk at the politician's claim. "The locals said, we are the owners," and refuse to acknowledge the politician's alleged land rights.

Walikale's main source of tin ore, the Bisie mine, accounts for a majority of the region's tin ore production and is controlled by the Congolese army. Military units also control access, forcing those transporting the minerals to pay money, food, or minerals to pass. "That's how the military people [get] rich."

Sometimes army and militia commanders accompany the minerals to the markets and warehouses where they are bought, avoiding intermediaries, all of whom will take a cut of the profits. "Commanders can go where they want and have access to money." If they're with the Congolese military, they can charter military planes to fly the minerals from the mines to Goma warehouses.

Controlling, limiting, or prohibiting the production of "conflict minerals" is a huge problem, Luanda acknowledges. He doubts that there's any effective way to prevent conflict. "Minerals have no color. You cannot know who they belong to." Unless the bags of ore are voluntarily tagged at the source, buyers can't know which minerals came from which mines, or who controls the mines. And voluntary cooperation is a fantasy, he says.

To foster small-scale, artisanal mining in Walikale, the miners have formed a mineral-buying cooperative, the Vin de Minier M'Pama du Bisie. Though miners "have no money to develop a co-op," it is a step toward self-determination. "The population is a victim of the presence of the military," not only at the Bisie mine but everywhere. "People are being asked to pay" portions of what they mine to whoever controls the mine, but this leaves nothing that might benefit the community at large.

Increasingly, villagers are demanding the right to impose taxes on mining so they can bring in commodities and services for their communities. To do this means taking the mines away from the armed groups, including the Congolese army. "Thousands of soldiers and military live off these mines and on the backs of the local people," Luanda says. People of eastern Congo are "victims of things they did not cause."

While some take faltering steps toward a civil society, fighting continues in eastern Congo much as it has for the past dozen years. Bandits erect roadblocks and loot. Militias battle over the mines. And communities have become involved in the fighting as war seeps ever deeper into civilian life. "Some are fighting for hills, very seriously, on a local level," he says, as mineral buyers seek exclusive rights to purchase minerals from certain regions. "Armed groups are not created for war," Luanda assures me, "but to give wealth to individuals or leaders. That's why they're created."

The Hutu militias that have occupied eastern Congo for fifteen years must be removed, says Luanda. The Rwandan government needs to let them return to Rwanda without fear of being killed by the Tutsis in revenge. So far, the Hutus have refused to go, claiming that "it's a question of life or death. We cannot go back to Rwanda when we have nothing to do [to make a living]."

"It's difficult," Luanda says about Rwandan president Paul Kagame's reluctance to let the *genocidaires* return to their country. "I don't know what isn't."

When I note that Kagame has at least agreed to open talks with the FDLR about their return, Luanda admits, "This is something positive."

Another step toward peace would be to confine Congolese soldiers to military barracks and bases. At present the soldiers roam freely, and since they're usually unpaid, they abuse women and steal food and liquor at gunpoint. Confining and controlling the soldiers "will help people to know how many soldiers there are," Luanda explains. If soldiers are confined to barracks except when on command missions, it will eliminate the confusion people feel when they encounter men in uniform. "If soldiers are seen, then people can ask, what's he doing here?" But "commanders don't want people to know [how many soldiers they have]," since they post their troops at mines to collect minerals and taxes.

The Battle of Bisie

Prince Kihangi Kyamwami, a member of the regional royalty, was born and raised in Walikale but moved to Goma twenty years ago for an education and a better life. "We came here to study," he says of his family. Now thirty, Kihangi is a lawyer and the author of a book about child labor in the mines of Walikale, *The Sad Reality of Child Labor in the Mines of Walikale: A Forgotten Crisis in the DRC.*

Although the Bisie mine is in Kihangi's home community, and despite the value of the minerals it produces, the community at large reaps nothing from it. The mine is controlled by the Congolese army; units of Hutu FDLR militia are also in the region. Hence "it is not possible to exploit the minerals" for the benefit of the community.

Fighting over minerals in the Walikale district began before the 1994 genocide, Kihangi says. He sees minerals as a curse, not a blessing. "Before the war, minerals were not known in the villages. At the time, we were doing agriculture, but we had no money."

Gold was mined in Walikale in the 1980s, and because of it, "many people came" hoping to mine it. Many stayed. "You don't think of going home" when you're making good money mining gold, Kihangi says. The subsequent discovery and development of tin, coltan, and tungsten brought a new wave of immigration to Walikale. "Now there are many minerals, but people don't know where [their new neighbors] are from."

Tin was first mined at Bisie in 2003, says Kihangi, after his uncle asked the government's Division of Mines to assay ore samples. Word quickly spread of the immense tin deposit. "People began to come from all over to work in the mines." In what was once a forested and sparsely populated land, the Bisie mine now supports some ten thousand people who live in the surrounding area in a mud and clapboard town where diseases like cholera are common. It is typical mining boom town, complete with hotels, bars, shops, and brothels, where everything under the sun can be purchased at exorbitant prices. Yet Bisie lacks roads and can be accessed only by footpaths jealously guarded by armed men and soldiers who extract "taxes" in exchange for security.

Mining has destroyed the traditional way of life that sustained people for eons in eastern Congo. "Everybody was attracted from the villages in the region and drawn away from agriculture. They can dig [in the mine] and get something to sell the same day," Kihangi says. "At the beginning, only heads of families would dig. But they [wanted] to produce more. So they started to bring in children. Some families moved from their homes to live at the mine. Children abandoned their schools."

Now entire families work in the mines while farming, raising animals, and other aspects of the culture, including education, are forgotten. Mining families now buy the crops and animals they need. But none of the money generated by the mine goes toward clinics, schools, or other community buildings. "It's very difficult to live" in a community that lacks basic facilities, he says.

Increasingly, children are sent into the mines instead of to school. Kihangi shows me photos of youngsters forced to work in the mines, including one of a child who had been beaten so badly he couldn't walk. The boy had been accused of not paying his so-called production tax to the soldiers who controlled the mine.

Such children are condemned to a lifetime of exploitation and poverty. "If things don't change, what is their future?" Kihangi asks. "It is another generation that is lost." Laws exist that require a 16 percent tax on mineral production, Kihangi tells me, of which two-thirds is supposed to be used for the construction of clinics, schools, and roads. "This has never been done."

Not long after tin mining began in earnest, the Bisie mine was captured by a local militia headed by a man named Samy Matumo. In the government's ongoing efforts to incorporate competing militias into the national forces, Matumo's men were made government soldiers and Matumo became a colonel. But Matumo refused to leave the area, considering Bisie his personal birthright, and began collecting what some estimate to have been hundreds of thousands of dollars each month from the miners and town merchants, not including the mine proceeds he commanded. Although Matumo was eventually forced out, little has changed today. The Congolese army's 85th Brigade now controls the mine. "They're doing the same thing as Colonel Matumo," says Kihangi, which is to exploit the Bisie mine.

On August 11 and 12, 2009, just days before I arrived in Goma, fighting erupted at the Bisie mine, killing more than a dozen and injuring about forty others. As the UN experts had reported and Kihangi confirmed, the 85th Brigade is composed of some Tutsi fighters who were part of the reconstituted army, who came with Rwandan army personnel. These Tutsi fighters stayed after the Rwandan army swept through the region earlier in the year, chasing the Hutu FDLR militia. Meanwhile, the Hutu FDLR also returned and is trying to muscle in.

The 85th Brigade was ordered to vacate the mine so that a private mining company could take over the operation, but the brigade hasn't budged. "They have complete control of the mine," Kihangi says, and have set up a permanent headquarters there. The soldiers refuse to relinquish control of the mine despite orders or legalities.

Kihangi is convinced that the government tolerates this situation because some officials are getting a cut of the mine production. "If the 85th Brigade gets money for itself, some money is sent to Kinshasa," he tells me. "There are generals in Kinshasa who are getting benefit from the mine in Bisie," and commanders of the 85th Brigade as well. "The government is also smuggling [minerals]," Kihangi says. "Since 2006, Bisie is like a jungle with no control."

Kihangi maintains that all of eastern Congo should benefit from the wealth produced by the Bisie mine, not just a handful of greedy politicians, the military, and militia leaders. "The whole country should benefit from the minerals at Walikale. Local people should benefit more. It could be possible if the mining laws were respected."

Kihangi's efforts to bring attention to the suffering of children and the whole community at the Bisie mine have been difficult and dangerous. "I was arrested and detained for two hours, explaining what I was doing." He shakes his head in dismay. "Nothing has been done at all to enforce the laws." Local and regional political authorities are involved in the mining in Walikale. "That's why there has been no change at all. International pressure is needed."

Kihangi's hope is that order can be imposed on the Bisie mine that will benefit the community and the miners, especially if it means replacing the crude manual mining methods now employed. "We think that if exploitation of minerals could be industrialized, change would come." But that would require a responsible company to come onto the scene.

A company called the Mining and Processing Congo (MPC), a consortium of South African and British investors headed by Brian Christophers, obtained title to the Bisie mine in 2006. But MPC has been unable to develop the mine because the Congolese military has not allowed its people access to the mine site. When they try, they've been greeted by bullets.

Nor do local miners like the idea of Christophers's MPC taking control of the mine. "There is tension between local miners and MPC," Kihangi admits, and MPC has been told to leave, since local miners fear the loss of their jobs and incomes. These fears, which company representatives say are baseless, have been fanned by members of the 85th Brigade as a means of prolonging their presence at the mine. Locals have armed themselves against this possibility, and this may have contributed to recent fighting. MPC is also viewed with suspicion because it has employed Rwandans. "We can't call it an armed group," Kihangi says of the largely unorganized locals.

Now all of community life revolves around the mine. "Only in places where there are no mines do children go to school." Without an educated populace, it is hard to find qualified people to lead the community, or to attract doctors, nurses, or teachers, or to find people qualified to represent the region in parliament who might bring pressure to bear on the government to change the situation. "Nobody is representing us," Kihangi says of parliament. "It is not our government. This can result in problems later on."

Kihangi believes the future of the Bisie and the Walikale district is bleak as he points to the demise of other mining communities. "In some places, when mines are finished, there is nothing else for kids to do but join the army." Joining the military does not provide much of a future. "The army doesn't care what their education level is, only what is their intention."

Kihangi concludes that the government should ensure that mining improves the community, and government officials should not be personally profiting from the mine. When the mine is played out, the people of Bisie will realize how badly they've been exploited. Deep resentment will develop, and if the community is trained militarily and armed, it will pose a threat to the government. "This is a kind of warning," Kihangi says. "In the future, we are sure there will be an explosion of war."

A Voice in the Wilderness

With its offices in Goma, the Mining and Processing Congo is between a rock and a hard place. Despite possessing exploratory rights to the

Bisie mine since 2006, MPC has been kept from the mine by the Congolese army, the entity that in most countries would be following orders from the government it is supposed to serve.

Jonas Sebatunzi is the legal adviser for MPC. We meet in a large open-air bar and restaurant in downtown Goma late one sunny, humid day in August 2009. The recent clashes at the Bisie mine have been between the 85th Brigade soldiers and a local militia, Sebatunzi tells me. The government forces are barely in control.

Then why doesn't the military enforce what the government had already agreed to do, which is turn over the mine to the MPC?

Sebatunzi shakes his head and says a lot of people benefit from the situation at the mine as it stands. "It's a long chain [to and] from Kinshasa." In 2003, the mine was under the control of the Ugandan-Rwandan force created in 1998, the Rally for Congolese Democracy, he says. The RCD refused to integrate into the national army, fearing they would lose both the mine and their lives due to the ethnic hatreds in the region. Inevitably, the Congolese military and its Mai-Mai allies took control of the mine in 2005, and it has remained in their grasp ever since. "Many artisanals are working there," says Sebatunzi, and the army's presence has done nothing to help the beleaguered miners. Each miner pays three or four days' worth of production to the army commanders while keeping just two or three days' worth of production for himself. The army also works with certain *négociants* who in turn sell only to certain *comptoirs*.

"The first time we tried to go there," Sebatunzi continues, "we were fired on by the military." The company turned to the government but quickly found that top officials in the region "have been involved themselves" in the plunder of the Bisie mine.

Nevertheless, Sebatunzi thinks that following prescribed procedures is the best path to follow. The company "wants government to gain complete control so we can begin to work there." But that must be preceded by an end to military involvement at the mine.

Is that possible, considering the endemic corruption in Congo?

Sebatunzi claims to have verbal assurances from President Kabila himself that the government will withdraw the military and install civilian mine police at the mine.

Sebatunzi shrugs when I ask if police can ensure peace and stability.

Perhaps, he says, if the latest round of deadly fighting can be sorted out. "We thought this [attack] had been done by the military themselves" as a way to justify their continued presence at the mine. One rumor is that the Congolese army provoked an attack by local Hutu FDLR militia, giving the army a reason to argue that the situation at the mine is too dangerous for the army to withdraw. Unfortunately, "it's not clear" what happened or why, even after weeks of investigation.

That the army would be loath to give up the mine is understandable, Sebatunzi says, since estimates are that ore valued at $300,000 to $500,000 per month is being taken from the mine. If that figure is accurate, the take amounts to about $6 million per year, about $100,000 per week or $15,000 per day. With that much value coming from the mine, it is no wonder MPC has trouble getting control.

Although the Bisie mine is just one of many mines in eastern Congo, Sebatunzi confirms that it produces the vast majority of cassiterite that comes out of the country. "Bisie is 80 percent of the activity," he says, and many buyers have a vested interest in maintaining their access. "They have their own lobby to keep the situation the way it is. If a company [such as MPC] gets control of the mine, they'll lose their share."

Meanwhile, the situation at Bisie continues to deteriorate. "They're destroying hills and forests. There's nothing for the local people. We think it's best for a company to take control of the mine." While this statement is clearly motivated by self-interest in part, Sebatunzi argues that the company is already under a microscope from local miners, government officials, military commanders, and the international community. If MPC assumes control of the mine, it will have no choice but to build infrastructure for the community. Left as it is, the community will never see any lasting benefits from the mine. "If miners are allowed to exploit the mine as it is now, there will be nothing left."

Sebatunzi agrees that mining in eastern Congo has brought a decade of bloodshed. "The violence is because of the minerals. Other areas are the same. The mines are feeding this kind of behavior." The solution is for the government to perform its duty. "The government must be strong to implement its authority so there is less violence." At Bisie, "little by little, they're imposing order," but the pace is dangerously slow; serious problems fester. "It cannot continue like this."

I mention that the miners at Bisie have formed their own cooperative. Is the company willing to work with them?

"We're not against cooperatives. The ideas are compatible. But [we] support cooperatives that are real. What kind of cooperative is it?" he asks, suggesting that the cooperative may not be a purely community-driven organization but could have backers with ulterior motives.

Regardless, Sebatunzi says his company can bring improvements for the miners and the community. "Now they're working under very difficult conditions. They don't have equipment. We can provide them with that."

While Sebatunzi tries to remain optimistic, he confides, "My impression is that the government doesn't know what is going on [at the mine]."

10

CONTROLLING THE FLOW

---

*C*OMPTOIRS ARE key players in the mining networks who move millions of dollars' worth of minerals out of eastern Congo and across East Africa to the ports of Mombasa, Kenya, and Dar es Salaam, Tanzania. From there, the minerals are shipped to Asian smelters, where they are refined into useable metals and sold to manufacturers for a wide range of uses in computers, mobile telephones, medical equipment, and devices such as hearing aids and pacemakers, jet engines and rockets, and even antilock brake systems.

On the front lines of the trade and lightning rods for criticism, *comptoirs* know the general origin of the minerals they buy and therefore are often accused of helping to finance the ethnic militias who have waged what has become the world's bloodiest conflict in the past sixty years.

Most *comptoirs* are not eager for public notoriety, fearing that they will become even greater objects of international scorn. One of Goma's most successful *comptoirs*, whom I call François because he declined to give me his real name, agreed to discuss minerals and their role in eastern Congo's decade of death.

François is a tall, well-dressed, and very composed Congolese mineral exporter who operates his business out of a converted home on a broad hill in Goma overlooking the placid waters of Lake Kivu.

On the fireplace mantel is an array of the metallic ores in which he deals: coltan, tin, and tungsten, among others.

"Coltan has brought another kind of life to Masisi," François says. It was first mined and sold out of the country by the *interahamwe*, the Rwandan Hutus who carried out the Rwandan genocide.

Comptoirs are just a cog in the wheel, he says, and he bristles when he and his fellow mineral buyers are blamed for the spread of bloody fighting that has plagued the region. He insists the war and the resulting bloodshed are not their fault, nor is the system of procuring, buying, and selling the minerals that has evolved over time.

War is the problem of the Congolese government, François says, which is well aware of what is going on in eastern Congo, including the business of mining and who controls it. The region's *comptoirs* pay hefty fees to the Congolese government for the right to do business there. His business buys an annual permit that costs $30,000. Once a permit is secured, "now you can buy the material" and prepare it for export.

François pays a tax on his exported minerals based on weight. Each purchase and sale is reported to the government, as required by law. François also pays other fees, and at the end of the day, the money goes to seven different agencies of government. Reliable transportation to truck the minerals to the eastern African seaports costs $230 per metric ton. It's an eight-hundred-mile trip, one way.

The Congolese government knows who the mineral buyers are and who the customers are, he says, because of the myriad details that must be reported for each and every transaction. These details include the banks where the money is deposited and the account numbers. "Nowadays, China is the biggest buyer," François says. "Sometimes [it is] South Africa."

François is mystified by complaints from the UN Group of Experts that it's difficult to follow the money trail for the buying and selling of eastern Congo minerals. "The UN report was very hard [on *comptoirs*]," he says. "We pay all this money to the government. The UN says they don't know where the money is going. The money is in circulation," which is where it should be, he says, flowing from buyers and processors to the miners and mining community.

François feels that mineral dealers in Goma and the South Kivu capital of Bukavu are targeted unfairly just because they work in eastern Congo. Dealers and buyers in neighboring Rwanda are just as deeply involved and may be even more culpable regarding funding, arming, and equipping the military units that control the flow of coltan out of the region. "When they say that mining is funding the war, they should look at the cause of the war." François points a finger at Rwanda. "They say it is blood coltan, but when it is in Rwanda, it is white," François says, suggesting that the "blood minerals" are effectively cleansed of the stigma by being moved through Rwanda. In fact, he suggests, Rwanda is thoroughly complicit in the eastern Congo minerals trade.

A pound of coltan ore is worth about $1.50, says François, which is the price paid to miners for the ore. About one hundred pounds would net a miner $150, a substantial amount of money for eastern Congo. If that money is spent foolishly, and whether or not it benefits the miners and the mining community, is not the responsibility of the *comptoirs* or *négociants*. Instead, "people need to be trained in money management."

Mineral buyers and exporters like himself provide a vital lifeline for many communities in the remote areas where the mines are located. The mineral buyers bring in money and supplies, providing remote communities with access to the outside world that most would never have otherwise. Because miners stop growing their own food and must buy what they need, even in remote areas, "food is very expensive," he says. "Why raise crops when locals can mine?" is the conventional thinking. Food and other goods are flown in, then the minerals are loaded and flown out. Unaccustomed to dealing in cash, most miners don't manage their money well. They typically sell their ore and spend the money until it is gone, then go back to the mines. The cycle is repeated endlessly, and many miners find themselves caught in a vortex of debt and borrowing based on their ability to keep mining.

François does not mention the Bisie mine and the community of miners that it supports, but he aptly describes the situation there. The phrase "eating like a miner" encapsulates the situation in eastern Congo. After they are paid, miners consume food and alcohol voraciously until all their funds are exhausted.

François has tried to help those in remote regions by providing them with picks, shovels, and bicycles. "I saw the conditions of people living near the mines," he says, with people sleeping on the ground without pads or blankets. These items were delivered on the condition that he would be paid back with a portion of the minerals that he collected on his return trip. "They took all of the equipment and they didn't come back," he says. "It's very difficult."

The *comptoirs* provide a vital service in the region because they deal with all groups of local society, most of which are involved in the mineral trade one way or another. "We are using small airplanes, [and] we take food to the population [in remote areas]," he says. In exchange, minerals are flown out. When the minerals are sold, the money flows through the system and business and people flourish. "Everyone is gaining something. The banks get millions."

François believes the Congolese government can do more to end the war in eastern Congo. The gap between the haves and the have-nots in eastern Congo is wide. Members of parliament earn $7,000 per month, while a public school teacher makes $30 per month.

Where does the money come from that pays these lavish salaries? I ask.

"All that money to the government is coming from the bush," François says, referring to the lucrative mineral production. Despite the millions of dollars generated by the region's vast mineral production, there is no "feedback" to the people except for what they can make through mining. Soldiers aren't paid and must turn to crime.

This makes for a huge amount of anger and resentment throughout society, argues François. "The population takes the money [from mining] for themselves" because "the government is doing nothing. The trouble is in our culture. [People] used to have many children because they were able to have a lot of land." With plenty of land, families could provide for themselves. But with more people migrating to cities, social unrest is brewing. The problem now is that families are still large and people "can always buy guns." The Congolese government needs to assert itself. "The country belongs to the government. The government should unify the country."

To blame mineral buyers and exporters for the country's problems is wrong, François says, when the government has the constitutional duty and means to solve the situation in eastern Congo. Mineral buyers and exporters should not be asked to make up for the government's failures. "It's not our fault. We follow the laws and we pay the tax. Out of that we are blamed [for] financing the war? I don't think it is true. People come to us with minerals and we buy," knowing that miners want to be paid for their labor.

Instead of addressing the desperate needs of the communities in eastern Congo, the government has become greedy, François says. Occasionally the government attempts to increase the mineral taxes and licensing fees, forcing the *comptoirs* to rebel because they know that higher fees enrich officials, not the people. The *comptoirs* fight fee hikes by going on strike and closing their operations. "We don't buy," he says. This upsets the miners, who don't get paid for their work and who in turn pressure the government to back off.

Since *comptoirs* are at the center of the process, it should be easy for them to identify the source of the minerals, I suggest. As various organizations have urged, this would allow minerals from conflict mines to be rejected, cutting funds to those who fight, loot, and rape.

François disagrees, saying that even if the minerals do come from conflict areas, neither *négociants* nor *comptoirs* can say for certain they know the origins because miners or the *négociants* can and do lie. "Nobody wants to tell the reality of where the minerals come from." Additionally, militia groups controlling conflict mines use local miners to sell the minerals for them, forcing them to lie about the origin of the minerals, using them carry the minerals to market and to collect the proceeds under the threat of death.

Turning the Corner

John Kanyoni speaks for most of the *comptoirs* in Goma, since he is a member of the Enterprise Federation of the Congo, the mining industry's equivalent of a chamber of commerce. I catch up with Kanyoni as he prepares for a meeting of the tin industry association, the International Tin Research Institute, which will later be known by the acronym ITRI. The association is meeting in Goma's finest hotel as part of an effort to develop an industrywide response to international pressure to stop the flow of money to the region's conflicts and conflict mines.

Kanyoni has a copy of the Global Witness report on his laptop and plans to use it as part of his presentation. As he projects the cover on the conference room wall, he complains about the report's use of a dramatic black-and-white photograph taken by British photographer Marcus Bleasdale of the brutal killing in eastern Congo. The image shows a couple of dead soldiers sprawled on the road outside of Goma. Kanyoni looks at me, shakes his head, and asks, "What does that have to do with buying minerals?" The Global Witness report is based on past events and ignores "all the achievements" by the members of the industry who "want to make sure our trading is not fueling the conflict."

The mineral dealers are aware of their responsibilities to lower the level of violence in the region, Kanyoni says. "We deal on a daily basis with *négociants*" who are in direct contact with miners and who in turn sell minerals to the *comptoirs*. Kanyoni and others in the business tell their *négociants* not to buy minerals that they know come from conflict mines. "Make sure you know that the minerals you are purchasing are not from mines controlled by armed groups." They insist that *négociants* are registered with the government, just as the *comptoirs* are, and want all miners, despite the vast number of them, also to register with the government. This will help the government and industry officials to know "exactly who [is] there." When they go to buy, *négociants* can then know they're dealing with registered artisanal miners and "avoid [dealing with] soldiers in the mines."

Kanyoni agrees that *comptoirs* must provide comprehensive records for mineral purchases. "Traceability is the key," he says, "traceability of finances and sales." This helps the government and others track the flow of money into and out of the region to determine if the money is going to armed groups. Although mineral buyers provide a vast amount of information about their activities, including monthly reports of their purchases and dealings, the government sits on the information, apparently unable or unwilling to process it. "We've asked the government to set up a network on how they can track that," Kanyoni says. So far, there's been little response.

While buyers want to work with the government, they also want the government to curtail the newly constituted army it has created in the field. The militias that were incorporated into the Congolese armed forces are the same units that have controlled the mines in the past. The government needs to withdraw these forces from the mining regions so that peaceful and legitimate commercial mining can continue. But this has been difficult. The Congo's prime minister, Adolphe Muzito, has been to Goma frequently in an effort to "clear up [the] situation." It hasn't worked, says Kanyoni.

When I ask about the Bisie mine, Kanyoni says the industry wants the army out of there and all other mining areas as well. But no military units have been moved and little has changed in recent months.

According to Kanyoni, the mineral buyers work with the UN's Group of Experts and with the US-based rights group the Enough Project, which also conducts an active campaign to ban the use of conflict minerals. "We are more concerned about human rights than you guys," Kanyoni says, although I'm not one of them. "I have people from my village who are refugees in Uganda" and who fled fighting in the region. Peace is a matter of personal and family urgency. "If we can prevent the use of armed groups, we are happy to do so."

The *comptoirs* oppose bans on the sale of minerals, because of the harsh impact this has on the small-scale, independent miners who are the vast majority of those digging the ore. If an embargo is imposed, "a lot of artisanal miners will be out of work." The loss of income hurts not only the miners but also their families and communities.

As a group, the *comptoirs* prefer an improved tracking and tracing method for minerals over an all-out ban, of course. "If we can't improve traceability, there will be no miners working eastern Congo," Kanyoni says. "Think about those artisanal miners. There are thousands of them." He and other mineral buyers are "open to any new ideas."

The ITRI, he says, has been blamed for the failure of the Congolese government to take control of the situation. But Kanyoni feels this is unfair. "There is not one single reason for them [the government] to say they're not in charge. The government has to play its role."

The mineral buyers, meanwhile, are doing their part. "We're paying taxes and giving jobs. We've achieved a lot with setting up new institutions," but he agrees that progress has been slow. "It has to be step by step" as the region emerges from twelve years of war. "It's a process. We can't get [to] everything in a very short time."

Still, Kanyoni believes that conditions are steadily improving. "They were killing people in Goma every day. But the situation is changing. We need to give a chance to government to establish its control. I see where we've come from, and where we are now. But we have a lot to do as well."

If the situation at the Bisie mine could be resolved in a civilized fashion, it might serve as an example for the region, I suggest. Does he support turning over the mine to MPC?

Kanyoni's response reveals the complexities and multiple motives behind the mining operations and the various interests at work in the region. "Bisie was an artisanal mine since 2001," he says. MPC worked hard to secure a permit from the government because of the "huge potential and high grade material" at the Bisie mine. The Congolese army's 85th Brigade has controlled it and plundered it, but the brigade has largely left the area. Now the buyers association "is putting pressure on the government so that any new army unit does not do that same thing."

But Kanyoni cautions against turning the mine over to MPC. "If they go back there, there is risk of an insurgency" because the local miners and others consider MPC to be outsiders who are not working for their best interests. "We've suggested that the government give [MPC] another concession and keep [Bisie] as an artisanal mine."

Although Kanyoni does not elaborate on why the group takes this position, there may be some self-interest behind it. If the region's largest source of tin ore is in the hands of an entity such as MPC, the company can work with the mineral purchasers it likes and bypass the rest. The company can also influence prices and percentages paid. Some of those currently getting rich from the mine could be cut out of the process.

What does Kanyoni see as the biggest obstacle to peace?

"It's important for the army to keep [newly integrated soldiers] involved and busy," he says, again throwing responsibility for the region's trouble onto the government's shoulders.

What about the Hutu FDLR militia?

Too much blame is being put on the FDLR as the source of the region's problems. "The actual percentage of mines controlled by the FDLR is very few. Almost nil."

Kanyoni should know, of course, but the significance of what he says is staggering. The Hutu FDLR controls almost no mines? If any mines are considered conflict mines, it would be FDLR mines. And now that the Tutsi CNDP militia is an official government force, the mines it controls are no longer conflict mines? Then who or what is to blame for the millions of dead and, more important, the ongoing conflict, if we have "almost nil" conflict mines? What happens to the veracity of the reports and claims of advocacy groups like Global Witness and the Enough Project that mining companies and electronics firms and their millions of consumers are funding millions of deaths? Are minerals and mining, then, really the cause of the killing?

Truth and Answers

Complaints about the government not taking control are almost universal. I find Gilbert Kalinda, a member of parliament from the

Walikale district, in his Goma office, which is in the process of being remodeled. He offers a far different view of the situation. Kalinda tells me of his recent trip to the United States on a government-to-government exchange program sponsored by the state department. He nods solemnly when I ask about minerals and war in eastern Congo.

"When we have war in the region, it begins in Goma," he says, "but the real target is Walikale." Similarly, "in Bunia [in the Ituri region], the war target is Mongbwalu [gold mine]." Once a mine is captured by a military group, "minerals support the war." The Bisie mine is by far the biggest prize in the region. Whoever controls it "gets a lot of money."

The *comptoirs* fault the government for the region's troubles, I say, and they argue that, as a group, they're improving things, not funding war.

Kalinda shakes his head and disagrees. "The buyers seem to encourage the system. They don't have a clear view of the origin of the minerals" and don't seem to want one. Identifying the source of minerals and banning conflict minerals would cut some out of the process. "It's up to them to know the origin of the minerals."

The government and others are "trying to have transparency" in the process, Kalinda says, regarding the origin, quantity, miners, and transporters as well as the *négociants* and *comptoirs*. The purpose is to "to discourage the rebel groups," specifically the Hutu FDLR militias, from fighting over the mines. But the militias circumvent detection by paying villagers to carry the minerals to market, sell them, and bring the money back to the rebel groups. They disguise the source of these conflict minerals. A more transparent process can help solve the problem, Kalinda believes. "When we can get clean buyers," then the militias will be indentified and "no one will buy minerals from them."

Kalinda recently met with the regional governor, and the two are encouraging *comptoirs* to reveal more about their business. Unless something is done to stop the sale of conflict minerals, the region faces an eventual ban on all ore purchases in eastern Congo. This would hurt Walikale. The government needs to be more forceful, but it also needs the cooperation and support of the commercial sectors. "The government must be supported by everyone."

An overarching problem is that the Congo lacks a sense of nationalism, Kalinda maintains. There's an attitude of every man for himself, which is why the *comptoirs* need to admit their role in fueling the wars in the region. "When you are a *comptoir*, and you have money to give to someone, and you give money to fuel war, you have a responsibility in this."

A detailed system is needed in which the source of ore coming out of the region is identified. "If you know this [ore] is registered, it's better to know where it is dug and what kind of organization he has."

The Hutu FDLR militia needs to be stopped, he says, since it is the major cause of fighting in the region. "To reduce the possibility of war is to reduce the possibility of the [FDLR] to get money." Artisanal mining cooperatives are an alternative to militias, Kalinda argues. "It can reduce the possibility that militias will use the minerals for war."

Kalinda points out that tin and coltan are just a couple of the minerals being mined from the region. Although not yet found in the Walikale district, uranium presents a stark contrast to the way most minerals are handled by the international community, he says. If uranium ore, which presents a global security concern since it is the base material for nuclear weapons, were handled as casually as other minerals from eastern Congo, people would be worried.

For example, the United States raised an alarm in 2003 when Iraq reportedly tried to obtain uranium from West Africa. If uranium were mined in eastern Congo and the current laissez-faire attitude toward minerals were applied, it would result in "not only war in Walikale, but war in all the world," Kalinda warns. "This would be dangerous to world security." Even though cassiterite and coltan don't present global security issues, he argues that the international community needs to "support the idea of transparency."

Kalinda understands the reluctance among eastern Congo businesses to accept regulation. "When there is no control for a businessman, it is a better situation. But it is better [for the community] to [have] control."

The *comptoirs* argue that to surrender control of their businesses to the government is no guarantee of peace or security, I say.

Kalinda agrees, but adds, "We don't know what's going on, on the ground. I realize it is part of the fault of the state," but knowledge of where minerals come from is necessary if the flow of money to the militias is to stop.

Despite the complaints from *comptoirs* of excessive reporting requirements, Kalinda contends that the government still does not know the extent of mine production in the region. "People should but don't know the statistics. How much is being taken out?" Truthful answers can help formulate a good policy. Ultimately, "this will give a better possibility to the people who are digging. Without attention from the government, [*comptoirs*] can do what they want."

Government involvement in the Bisie mine has done nothing to improve the situation, I suggest, and has only changed the names of who is getting rich from it.

The government is promoting artisanal mining at Bisie, Kalinda responds, despite the fact that MPC demands its mining rights. Kalinda suspects that MPC may have instigated the recent violence at Bisie so it could be allowed to take over. But the Bisie miners don't trust the company and fear that with a private company in control, they will not make as much money. "Suddenly [a miner] sees someone coming [who] says, I own this mine and control the area." The miners have faced this claim repeatedly and are tired of it. "People are frustrated." MPC wants a monopoly at the Bisie mine, Kalinda says, but in fact has only exploratory rights. "People are afraid the company will come and chase them away." Instead, "the people want to chase the company away."

Because of the tenuous situation at Bisie, Kalinda argues that putting the Congolese army in control is good, at least for the short term. "It is best to organize security with the military," he says, but "we can't stay with the military. With the mining police, it is better." The army presence "gives the impression of war."

War is the reality in the region, I say. Since the military has been in control of the Bisie mine for so long, will it voluntarily relinquish control?

Kalinda smiles and nods. "All it takes is an order."

His comment suggests that the government is in control. The *comptoirs* say no. Kalinda is also saying that the *comptoirs* run the show, while the *comptoirs* say no. Instead, they suggest that politicians wistfully watch the exploitation and wait for chances to muscle their way in.

Few share Kalinda's confidence in the government. Some suggest that if the government wants peace in eastern Congo, it needs to involve mining communities in the structure of government. The government needs to become inclusive, not exclusive. Most communities are isolated and therefore vulnerable, forcing them to turn to armed ethnic groups for protection and for a sense of community and control.

A Geologic Scandal

My translator and fellow journalist Jacques Kahorha and I return to the North Kivu provincial assembly after our meeting with Gilbert Kalinda. Nearly two years earlier I visited militia groups in North Kivu to discuss the ill-fated Goma agreement.

We meet with Benito Kansuli Kiezele, a representative from the Lubero region, the gold mining community about 125 miles north of Goma. It struggles with the same dilemma faced by communities throughout eastern Congo.

"It took all our wealth from the region," he says of gold mining. "But [the mining companies] didn't build any infrastructure," so the region still lacks roads, schools, and clinics. There's little opportunity to attend school, so most young people turn to mining or agriculture. "It's a sad situation."

A Canadian company has approached the community about reopening a mine in the Lubero area, but "people are not confident in the company because of the past," Kiezele says. "Most locals seem not to support this company in this area. They want to get some guarantees."

Villagers face a dilemma, he says, because they know that artisanal mining will never generate sufficient revenue to build the schools and clinics the community needs.

"The problem with the $200 or $300 [the miners] get [is that it] still can't fix the roads. So things stay the same." The wish is that "some funds can come back to the people" so that mining benefits the community at large. Instead, "nothing changes on the ground, despite the presence of minerals. People don't get the benefit of the minerals."

Companies that profit from the region's mines should return a portion to the community, he says. "If there is a company that can work with minerals, it can also build roads, schools, and buildings."

As communities struggle with their situations, it has been easy for armed groups to recruit, says Kiezele. The Mai-Mai Simba militia in his area has been attracting new members, in part because the Hutu FDLR is trying to take over gold production there.

Besides gold, coltan is also now being exploited, he exclaims with a frustrated shrug. "Coltan attracts so many armed groups. If there were no minerals, we would not have this problem. We are victims of a geologic scandal."

Father Alfred Ndrabu in Bunia.

Warning written in blood on schoolroom wall, Bogoro village.

Skulls and bones from massacres at Bogoro.

Bogoro villagers talk about the past.

Mining for gold, knee-deep in mud, Mongbwalu.

Gold mining in Mongbwalu.

A gram of gold.

Pluto village.

Children of Pluto.

Kiiza Badja, right, with neighbors, Pluto village.

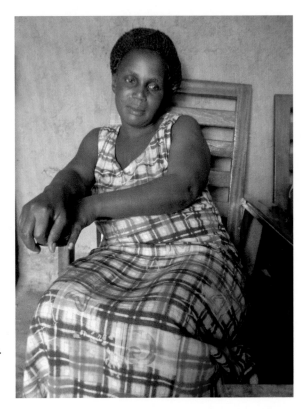

Leanne Uzele, Pluto.

Devote Musafire, rape clinic
counselor, Goma.

Cow herd in Dinka territory, South Sudan.

Coltan mine, Bibatama village.

Coltan miners, Bibatama.

Bibatama villagers.

Coltan miners, Bibatama village.

Disputed coltan mine near Bibatama.

Coltan panned from washed ore.

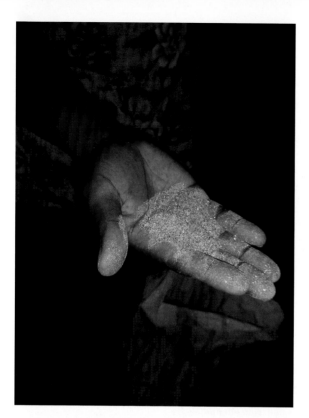

Handful of coltan, Goma miners' cooperative.

Primo Pascal, television journalist, Goma.

Distribution of flour, Goma refugee camp.

Girls with firewood bundles, Goma refugee camp.

Distribution of cooking oil, Goma refugee camp.

Refugee camp, Goma.

Door made from cooking oil cans.

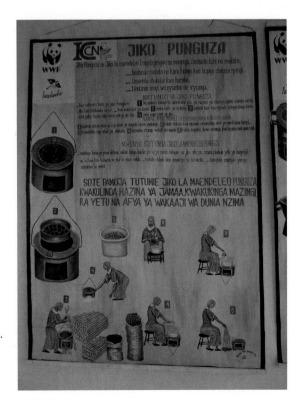

Poster urging efficient use of fuel.

Refugee Esther Murikatete shows the gunshot wound to her shoulder.

War widows of Rutshuru.

Didier Bitaki, Mai-Mai militia commander.

Woman toting charcoal out of Virunga National Park, near Goma.

Woman carrying child and charcoal from Virunga National Park, near Goma.

Boys selling charcoal at edge of Virunga National Park.

11

INTO COLTAN COUNTRY

MILITIAS THAT control the mines don't like to accommodate foreigners, especially journalists who wander around, take pictures, and interview people. Erecting roadblocks, collecting fees, harassing travelers, and in some cases kidnapping are more their style. Shortly after my arrival in Goma, Kahorha tells me about a Congolese television journalist who recently was beaten and barely escaped alive when he tried to visit a coltan mine.

That's what I need to do, I say, despite the risk. Kahorha only shakes his head.

When we were wrapping up our meeting with François, the Goma *comptoir*, we brought up the possibility of visiting a coltan mine. François said that of course we could visit a mine and mentioned the same one where the journalist had been beaten. Kahorha laughed and said thanks, but no. François was puzzled until Kahorha explained why. François then dismissed our concerns, saying that the incident was just a misunderstanding. He made a call.

A couple of days later, we pick up Alphonse, a lanky and affable man in his late twenties, who is related to the village chief and who has arranged our visit to the mine, high in the Masisi mining district and deep in the heart of coltan country. The seasonal rains have lingered, leaving parts of Goma black and muddy, a by-product of the volcanic rock on which the town is built. We are on the road early, wary of the torrential downpours that can turn the mountain roads into slick and treacherous tracks.

After we snake through Goma's back streets, Alphonse directs us to a busy thoroughfare, where we pull to the side in the midst of a market. He jumps out and disappears down an ally. Ten minutes later, Alphonse reappears with an armful of thick jackets. When I ask why, Kahorha tells me that it will be cold where we are headed. "It's a different climate." I am more than a little skeptical, since I can see the dark and distant hills and there is not a snowflake in sight. But this is Africa.

We race along the road out of town, rolling across flatlands, and soon angle our way higher into the Masisi hills. Kahorha recounts a former trip into this same territory accompanying a BBC reporter who was covering the fighting between government forces and the fractured Tutsi CNDP militia that controlled the region. They stopped at the final government checkpoint at a spot that we had just passed and were allowed to continue into rebel country—at their own risk. They managed to contact the militia, get the story, and return unharmed.

Our trip is not quite so tense, he assures me, and at the moment I can only agree. In fact, the trip feels more like a journey into a mythical land than into a war zone. I gaze at the misty and deeply verdant hills, impossibly steep, yet covered in a patchwork of vegetable plots hacked out of the hillsides by hard labor and calloused hands wielding thick-bladed hoes.

For the next two hours we negotiate switchbacks, steadily and relentlessly climbing the sticky roads while eyeing the low-hanging clouds. It has rained every day I've been in Goma, even though Kahorha insists that it's the dry season, a term I have a hard time applying to the weather. I can accept, however, that the Masisi district has a unique climate, politically speaking. For years the region has been the stronghold of the Congolese Tutsi general Laurent Nkunda and his CNDP army, said to be the biggest impediment to peace in eastern Congo.

But I wonder, with him now erased from the equation by the Rwandan government, is the area on the brink of normality?

The ride gives me time to ponder what minerals and mining have meant to the people here, who have been caught up in a vortex of violence and who advocacy groups contend are victims of greedy corporations and the voracious appetites of global consumers. The image created is one of hapless villagers sitting on mountains of ore being fought over by capitalist warmongers bent on wringing billions of dollars in profit from their flesh and blood. What is this stuff that they call coltan, anyway? It is not until I return to the United States that I will be able to sort fact from fiction and answer that question.

Coltan is verbal shorthand for two metals closely related in their physical properties: columbium, also called columbite, and tantalum, also called tantalite. The two metals are found together, and it's normal for them to be deposited where tin ore is found. For many years tantalum was a by-product of tin smelting. Although columbium/columbite was renamed niobium (Nb) in 1949, it was discovered in the very early 1800s by a British scientist who found it in a chunk of ore that came from the United States, and its old name has persisted. Tantalum (Ta) was discovered at about the same time in Sweden and named after Tantalos, a character in Greek mythology, the father of Niobe, after whom niobium was named. Tantalos was condemned to stand in water with luscious fresh fruit dangling above him. This myth is the origin of the word *tantalize*, because the fruit was always just beyond his grasp, and each time he bent for a drink, the water receded. Tantalos's daughter, Niobe, is the goddess of tears. The myths are appropriate for eastern Congo; the valuable ores have tatalized the Congolese but have brought mostly grief.

What's so special about coltan? Both tantalum and niobium have extremely high melting points, over five thousand degrees Fahrenheit. Coltan is virtually impossible to corrode, has superconductivity, and can handle a huge electrical charge. And it is easily mixed with other metals such as tungsten, molybdenum, and titanium. About 60 percent of the world's tantalum goes into electrical capacitors used by the electronics industry. These capacitors regulate the flow of electricity within integrated circuits and are found in mobile phones, video cameras, and laptop computers. Because it doesn't corrode, tantalum is used for chemical processing equipment but also for nuclear reactors, aircraft engines, and missile parts. It is impervious to body fluids, so it is used in medical and surgical applications such as metallic implants. It goes into special glass with high refractive qualities, making it ideal for camera lenses and very thin lenses on personal eyeglasses. When combined with carbon and graphite, it becomes one of the hardest materials known and is used for the cutting edges of high-speed tools.[1]

A valuable material for today's technology, obviously. But what does this have to do with eastern Congo? I contact the Tantalum-Niobium International Study Center in Lasne, Belgium, about that. Despite the vast amount of fighting and death associated with mining in eastern Congo, for the past sixteen years the Congo and its neighbors have been very minor players in the world's supply of tantalum and niobium, providing only about 10 percent. This also applies to the Congo's known but yet unmined tantalum reserves, which are routinely and wrongly said to be the biggest in the world. "In addition, known and likely resources of tantalum in the [Congo] are relatively minor compared to the rest of the world—far from the oft quoted figure of 80%, they are, in fact, closer to 9% of the world resources," the center says.[2] South America has 41 percent of known tantalum reserves, followed by Australia with 21 percent. China and Southeast Asia and Russia and the Middle Eastern countries each have 10 percent. Central African countries have 9 percent, and other African countries have 7 percent. The rest is found in North America and Europe.

In fact, more tantalum is recycled and comes from secondary sources such as tin smelting than is mined in all of central Africa. Since 2000, Australia has been a primary supplier of tantalum, and from 2003 to 2007 it had the lion's share of the market. In 2009, that changed, and now Asian and South American countries are the major sources, followed by the Congo and its neighbors.

When looking at the value of all of the minerals coming out of eastern Congo, the study center says that gold is much more important, amounting to about 55 percent of the total exported mineral value. Tin makes up about 41 percent of exported mineral value, followed by tantalum at about 4 percent and tungsten at a measly 1 percent.[3]

I find similar statistics about the volume of tin ore that actually comes out of the Congo from the international tin association, ITRI, based in St. Albans, United Kingdom, considered the world's foremost authority on the tin industry.[4] Eastern Congo has been an extremely minor source of tin for the world's supply, generating only about 1 to 2 percent annually of the total supply going back to 1980. The amount increased to about 5 percent from 2005 to 2008. According to ITRI, China and Indonesia provide about 65 percent of the world's supply of tin. Another 20 percent or so comes from Bolivia and Peru. About 10 percent comes from elsewhere around the world, leaving the final 5 percent to come from eastern Congo and its neighbors.[5] Tin ore, as mentioned, is also important to the electronics industry because it is light, conducts electricity nicely, and has replaced lead for use in electronics circuitry in all manner of devices.

Considering that just 5 percent of all tin comes from eastern Congo, the region is certainly not critical to the world's tin industry, and given the controversies swirling around minerals coming from the region, mining there may not be worth the hassle. Tin from the Congo is even less significant to the electronics industry since more and more tin is being recycled, lessening the need for raw ore. Considering that 5 percent or less of all tin comes from the eastern Congo, Congolese tin has a 5 percent or less chance of ending up in electronics components.

This data contradicts the campaigns of advocacy groups, who rightly want to end the horrific bloodshed and violence in eastern Congo but do so by claiming that much of the tin, tantalum, and tungsten used by electronics industry pays for the war in eastern Congo. Is the Congo's tin and coltan critical to the global electronics industry? Is it critical enough to send global corporate giants stampeding to the mines of North and South Kivu, dispensing satchels of dollars and euros to any and all militia fighters they can find? Hardly. Despite the very small role that Congolese tin and coltan play in the global market, the money these minerals generate is hugely significant to eastern Congo. That significance can be counted in the millions of dollars and millions of lives lost or damaged over the past sixty-five years in the worst human death toll since World War II.

To a Coltan Mine

By late morning we crest one of the bigger hills and park, leaving our driver with the vehicle. Luck is on our side as the sun breaks through and the skies clear, leaving only a high, thin layer of clouds. We don our jackets despite the warm weather and hurry down the hillside following a grass-covered road.

We're soon surrounded by a cluster of young boys and girls who fall in behind, shouting "*muzungu*," the Swahili word for foreigner, usually a white man. I feel like the Pied Piper. Kahorha teases them about being afraid of a *muzungu*, then tells them somewhat proudly that I am from America, which "is where money comes from." They tell him that's where they want to go. Kahorha says I will take them.

More than halfway down the steep hillside, we come to a fenced compound overlooking the village of Bibatama, a scattered community of mud houses with corrugated metal roofs. The surrounding hills are neatly cultivated squares of beans, corn, and vegetables. At the village chief's house we are shown into a room furnished with couches and overstuffed chairs. We're told to sit and wait, since chief Bazingo Kabano is out in the field with his cows. But we're not to worry. Someone has gone to find him.

We are offered fresh, warm milk, but I decline, fearing the worst for my digestive system. I apologize, saying I don't feel well, and watch as Kahorha and Alphonse gulp down large cupfuls.

Chief Kabano soon enters, and we shake hands as he settles into a large chair. Kabano, an unassuming man, wears a coat, mud-splattered pants, and rubber Wellingtons. I explain that I want to see the village's coltan mine and take some pictures. He readily agrees, saying he's glad that I've come. The coltan mine, he says, began as a tin mine owned by a foreign company that no longer operates in the area. With the discovery of coltan, the mine was reopened.

We trek across the grassy hillside with least twenty men and an equal number of children. At the base of a steep slope is a muddy, wriggling stream that snakes into the distance. That small river continues for some twenty-five or thirty miles, Kahorha says, and is the source of coltan mined by the residents all along the winding river valley. The hills are scarred with many mines similar to the one I'm about to see, he says, and are the region's primary source of wealth—and the cause of violence and bloodshed.

Kabano's father worked in the mine when it produced cassiterite, he says. When word spread that the region might have coltan, his father had the minerals tested, confirming that this was true. The community obtained a permit from the government and restarted the mine. He estimates that 1,500 to 2,000 artisanal miners work in the nearby hills.

As we round a hump on the slope, the small mine appears, a vertical gash in a hill exposing red and white rock and mud. Half a dozen men are working, wielding picks and pointed steel bars. Kabano shouts at them to get busy, sending them into a frenzy of action.

I watch as several young men jab at a section of white, crumbly granitic rock with the steel rods while others scoop up the rock by hand or with a shovel, dumping it into bags. A trickling stream has been diverted by a ditch cut across the hill, and its water is used to wash red clay off the rock, which is then crushed and panned, much like gold. The heavy coltan settles to the bottom of the mining pans. Once collected, it's the consistency of coarse and dense black sand. As I step back, the frenzy stops. How can these men make any money with such sporadic work? I ask.

"This is quite different here," Kabano explains. Everyone in the village must work in their fields at least one day a week. This happens to be that day. If he didn't impose this rule, he says, most of the miners would abandon agriculture altogether. It's a critical problem for the region, because once the miners start making money, they stop growing food, and Kabano fears that his community will lose its traditional self-reliance. He fears his friends and neighbors will become dependent on mining, squander their money, and let their farms lie fallow. "It's easy here to have and grow beans, corn, and such," he says. "Mines have an end."

To continue agriculture, some villagers are paid to farm and raise animals rather than work in the mine, ensuring that the community has fresh food as well as money from the mine. "The money from here we give to people to cultivate," he says, gesturing toward the mine. "The village has regular meetings where they encourage people to cultivate. We tell people they have fertile lands and it can't stay still." If villagers resist, then individual owners must let their land be grazed communally.

As Kabano talks, I gaze at the telecommunications tower on top of a distant hill. I point to it and ask him about it, noting that mobile phones are one of the uses of the coltan that he mines. Is he worried about the complaints from advocacy groups that the international companies who buy the ore are fueling the fighting that has decimated the region for the past dozen years?

Kabano shrugs. "Many companies in the United States and the European Union are getting rich. But for us it's not a problem here because money from the coltan pays for school fees and food." He smiles proudly and explains that the coltan has made some villagers rich. "These people have houses in Goma." More important, he says, this mineral and this technology allow him and his villagers to connect to the outside world.

Kabano doesn't mention the fighting that has plagued the region.

If the mine is such a good thing, I ask, why is there so much fighting?

Again he shrugs. "We can not know [the answer to] this," adding that in eastern Congo, "minerals are helping the Congo and a lot of other countries."

Kabano accompanies me up the steep hillside and back to our vehicle, a walk of about thirty minutes. Kabano hands me a small plastic bag of black coltan grit, about the size of a large marble. I am amazed at its weight. I thank him, not knowing what I'm going to do with it, and we say good-bye.

The clouds have gathered again as we head down the mountain. As I gaze at the wisps of fog hanging above the trees and heft the tiny bag of coltan, I hold the source of years of conflict that has claimed many lives. A very small portion of this mineral may have found its way into the world markets, and perhaps even into the portable telephones that all of us carry. For such a minuscule amount, there has been so much bloodshed. The disproportion feels strangely haunting.

Alphonse returns with us to Goma, and as we carefully descend the red clay roads that cut through the verdant terrain, I ask him if there has been fighting in and around the village. Yes, he says with a shrug, as if it's a given fact. Nkunda's CNDP militia controlled the area and his village for many years, including the mining. Helicopters brought weapons in and took coltan out, he says. The CNDP did not mine the ore but had the locals dig it. The CNDP then taxed it by taking a portion or demanding money. Ore taken by the miners was trucked to Goma, where it was also "taxed" by the government through fees charged the miners. Everyone made money, including the combatants, and nobody objected. "We were happy with the CNDP. They were the saviors of this area."

How much coltan was taken?

"A lot," he says with a smile.

Some of the heaviest fighting he remembers took place in July 2008 when the government forces attacked Nkunda's forces, prompting vicious counterattacks.

Over the years, how many people were killed in the village?

Alphonse shakes his head slowly. "So many people died. It is too painful to talk about. We can't count the number of people who died."

Bags and Backrooms

Co-operama is a miners' cooperative, formally known as the Cooperative for Exploitation Artisanal Miners du Masisi. Its gritty, concrete office is noisy in the early morning as I talk with the co-op's general director, Jotham Vwemeye. Dozens of Masisi's miners mill around the office entrance and inside, waiting to be paid for the ore they've dropped off in the back room.

The miners' cooperative doesn't fit with the images conjured up by the phrase "conflict minerals." That phrase suggests that miners and their families, friends, and villagers are the victims, not the beneficiaries, of the industry.

Is Vwemeye comfortable dealing in what the outside world now calls conflict minerals?

"This is not the case," he insists with a shake of his head. "Locals bring the minerals to us, and they sell them to us." Foreign corporations are not exploiting the miners. Exploitation is being done by the Congolese civilians and military officials who claim rights to the land where the minerals are.

When a bag of ore comes into the office, how does the co-op know that the minerals do not come from mines controlled by militias? How does he or the other co-op members know the difference?

"This is not the case with us," Vwemeye says again. The co-op was formed "to protect the interests of the members." Beginning in 2004 with fifty members, it now has three thousand members. A former miner himself, Vwemeye now prefers to help other miners. The co-op influences the Goma coltan market by working to keep mineral prices high. If prices drop, the co-op sits on its stockpiles of coltan and waits for the price to climb. If the co-op didn't use such tactics, the miners would be at the mercy of the buyers who "go to the villages and [pay] the prices they want."

Despite years of digging the ore and selling it, the lives of the miners throughout the region did not improve. "We decided to put the artisanal miners together to defend their rights," Vwemeye says. "The cooperative is a means of improving the lives of people at a local level." The idea is to plow the profits from the co-op back into the communities where the minerals originate. He is optimistic about the co-op's future and its ability to grow in influence. "We sense that war is ending and we can be operational. We are expecting to bring building materials to the villages" so that schools can be built and roads improved.

The co-op operates like any other mineral-buying organization, Vwemeye says, and deals with most of the *comptoirs* in the region. The co-op has its own *négociants* who travel throughout Masisi buying minerals that are then stored in its Goma warehouse. The *négociants* of the co-op then sell the minerals to the *comptoirs*, but only if the price is right.

Fighting in the Masisi region has been a problem, Vwemeye concedes, as control of the mines has changed hands. Often "we have to leave the area," but lately the situation had improved. "Since the clashes are over, we go back and resume agriculture and start digging [for minerals]. [As] peace is restored, it is easy for us to resume. During war it is difficult to work. If peace is restored, people can work well."

Vwemeye supports the government's efforts to bring peace, because they improve everyone's prospects for the future. "We think peace is there now," he says of Masisi, because people can travel freely back and forth to their villages.

But peace never seems to last, I suggest.

"To say that peace is precarious" is accurate, but peace or the lack of it is not because of the minerals in the ground, he insists. "[War] does not depend on us. You can see how government is investing in peace. That is the confidence we have." Co-op members are expanding their operations, he says proudly. "Today we're going deeper [into the countryside] to meet with miners on how we can build our activities." Again, he says, "Peace does not depend on us."

Mining in the midst of war means working with militias. This requires that miners share minerals and the proceeds with armed groups, I say. Since the government forces now control Masisi, having incorporated the former Tutsi CNDP militia into the national army, the co-op must have ties with these forces.

It's a necessary evil, he says. "It is normal to have a good relationship with government. We work with the ministry of mines and the division of mines." To the extent necessary, the co-op attends government and mining association meetings and files its reports. "We know they're under the charge of the government," he says of mining officials. "We cooperate with the mine police in the area. They look at what is done on the ground."

Vwemeye leaves for a meeting, turning me over to Theodore Mutazimiza, one of the co-op's *négociants*, who works with the Masisi coltan miners. One of the co-op's programs teaches the miners how to manage their money. "We train them how to save money. At the end of a period, they see the money and are very happy." This is a dramatic change from past behavior, since "before, they would spend all they had." Miners drag sacks of ore to the market and sell it for what they can. It is not unusual for the co-op to have over a ton of ore on hand and ready for sale. "Then, it is easy to sell for a lot of money."

The co-op has simplified the mineral-buying process, Mutazimiza says. In the past, *négociants* went to the countryside to buy minerals, but now miners usually bring the minerals to the co-op.

Although the miners did not organize until 2004, the region's *négociants* organized in 1989, Mutazimiza says. "We noticed a change when we organized," which is why they helped form the mining co-op. If the *comptoirs* went on strike, it shut down the system. Because the *négociants* couldn't hoard the minerals themselves, "we were obliged to stop working" whenever the *comptoirs* stopped buying. But with a co-op, the miners and the *négociants* are able to continue mining and selling regardless of the *comptoirs*, he says. Some former miners advance to become *négociants*. "This is something positive for us."

This positivism is nice to hear, but haven't minerals destroyed the communities in Masisi?

Mutazimiza says war is a problem but the miners have persevered. "War came after we started our organization in 1989. War could not stop us." Over the years, the miners and the *négociants* have worked together to help each other through the darkest of times. "Where there is war, miners and *négociants* lose their property. The cooperative is a way to stabilize [this]. The cooperative is [the miners'] property. The war in Masisi is due to the rebellion in the area," not the minerals, he insists.

Of course, when the CNDP took control of Masisi, Mutazimiza says, "we lost a lot of money. Taxes were paid to both the CNDP and the government. The loss we had is due to that period. We had to pay double taxes for the same goods." The miners and *négociants* paid the Tutsi CNDP militia $100 per truckload of coltan at checkpoints throughout the Masisi district. Most of the miners preferred to keep working despite the war and double taxes, saying, "If we do nothing, our communities will die." Mutazimiza shrugs at the memory, saying, "Taxes are common for other activities."

I ask about the controversy over the ownership of the mine at the Bibatama village I just visited. Mutazimiza explains that a member of parliament who was once a *négociant* from the region and a former co-op member claims rights to several mines around the village. The man had been given a parcel of land to mine, just ten yards by twenty yards, and got the proper permits. Unsatisfied with the parcel, he wanted to mine the river bottoms, which were loaded with coltan, and struck a deal with the CNDP to help protect his claim. When his permit expired, he obtained a renewal from government officials in Kinshasa, then returned to the village and claimed that he now had rights to all minerals in the valley around the village.

"People said, no. You can't say that you have bought our land. Who did you talk to?" Complaints were filed with the government and investigators were sent, Mutazimiza says. The mining claim is now on hold. The situation is complicated, because Congolese law requires that miners taking minerals from someone else's land must pay the landowner. The issue now is over who has legal claim to the land, Mutazimiza maintains.

As we talk, men are moving in and out of the co-op, so I ask to see the action in the back room. Mutazimiza pushes back his chair and I follow him through a narrow hall that opens into a cramped room scattered with bags of gritty, coarse sand of various colors. The room is quietly busy and the talk is calm and serious, punctuated by an occasional shout of laughter.

At one wall is a scale with a hook on which bags of ore are hung and weighed. Mutazimiza unties a bag and thrusts his hand into it, extracting a palmful of silvery sand. This is the prize, the coltan that makes its way to other continents to be processed, refined, and eventually transformed into components for the mobile phones that many of the miners in the room carry in their pockets.

Bane of Bibatama

My experience in the village of Bibatama with Chief Kabano was peaceful, and I have a tiny bag of coltan to prove it. But it had been a much different visit for television journalist Primo Pascal just a few weeks earlier, when he was attacked at the village. Pascal is the head of programming for the national television station in Goma and an acquaintance of Kahorha's. We find Pascal in his office on a hill overlooking Goma, and he explains that the member of parliament who has claimed the mineral rights in Bibatama valley has a document that allows him to explore and access all of the land in the community.

I think of the similar document held by the Mining and Processing Congo company for the Bisie mine, which is of little use.

"Local people have never accepted anyone to do [mining at Bibatama]," Pascal says, and the member of parliament has no one on his side there, although he's promised to fix the road to the village.

Kahorha notes that we walked that same road, now covered with grass. Chief Kabano didn't want that road improved because it would mean trucks passing by his house each day and he didn't want the noise and dust. It seems reasonable.

The miner's co-op is also resisting any takeover of the Bibatama, Pascal says. They don't want the profits going to someone who is already in a position of privilege, such as the member of parliament.

The man has been relentless, however, Pascal says, and "is trying to get people to agree that they will benefit from his claim." He proposes that the Bibatama mine be mechanized, and if the community allows that, then improvements can be made in the village. Regular wages will be paid. But the miners fear that if machines are brought in, they'll be pushed out.

The member of parliament has backers for the mining operation but needs agreement from the community. He asked Pascal to make a documentary on the community and the mine at Bibatama for government officials and potential investors.

"When people heard I was from Goma and making a documentary, they came with sticks," Pascal says. The crowd quickly grew to two hundred people, some armed with machetes. "It was only [by] luck that they didn't get the camera and wound us. Our car was hit with stones" as he and his crew fled.

Hostilities in the area are driven by the same ethnic problems that have caused most of the violence in eastern Congo. "There is a problem in this area between Hutus and Tutsis," Pascal says, and because of that, "it's hard for [the parliament member] to establish himself."

The village of Bibatama is ethnic Hutu and the member of parliament is an ethnic Tutsi. Although the larger area is controlled by the former Tutsi CNDP militia that is now part of the national army, villages such as Bibatama are still defended by the local PARECO militia, Pascal says. Although the member of parliament "was given a guarantee that there would be no conflict" between PARECO and the former CNDP units, the Bibatama villagers still don't want an outsider controlling their mine.

"The area is still under the control of armed groups" despite the tenuous peace. The miners have threatened to take up arms if the member of parliament tries to take control, Pascal says. Any of these groups "can take up guns at any time. Peace is precarious. You can't say stability is established in the area. You can't say who is controlling what."

Additionally, some former fighters from the Tutsi CNDP and from PARECO have refused to join the national army. These renegade militiamen are still armed, still roaming around, and can quickly destabilize the situation.

Pascal falls silent, looking somewhat confused, distant, and sad, as we both wonder if the region can ever have peace.

12

REALITIES OF REFUGEES

HIGH CLOUDS soften the equatorial sun as Kahorha and I head for one of the many refugee camps outside of Goma. Kahorha wants to show me the work that his nonprofit group does for refugees. Called Action Santé Femme (Women's Health Action) and known by the acronym ASAF, the organization works with the international aid organization Oxfam to provide fresh water to the refugee camps around Goma. The one we visit is known as Magunga 3.

The water source is nearby Lake Kivu, where a pumping station has been built on the shoreline property of a monastery. The water is drawn out of the lake and pumped several miles to the camp's metal holding tanks, perched on mounds, from which it flows to scattered concrete washing and drinking pads. The group also manages clusters of outdoor toilets that are critical for maintaining sanitation for the tens of thousands who are crammed onto the sharp-edged lava rock. "Being a journalist is good," Kahorha says, "but you can do a lot more to help people. That is why I got involved."

We pause to watch one of the regularly scheduled food distributions. The food is barely enough to fend off starvation: a medium-sized sack of flour per person per month, a bucket of beans, and a container of vegetable oil per family. Flour is scooped from large white sacks into smaller ones and cooking oil is poured from large silver tins stamped

"USA" in blue flanked by red stripes. The tin canisters are as popular as the oil. They're cut, pounded flat, and used to make doors for the small huts, which are elongated domes made of sticks, branches, and leaves and covered with white plastic tarps provided by the United Nations. The metal doors, Kahorha says, provide scant security for the single and widowed women, all of whom are vulnerable to rape.

We stop at a large open-air tent where small clay stoves are stacked on shelves to dry in the damp air. The clay stoves make efficient use of the limited supply of firewood. The stoves are foot-high clay cylinders with round metal collars that concentrate the heat under a cooking pan. Wood or charcoal is fed into an opening at the bottom. The stoves serve yet another purpose. Women are the main wood gatherers and must go ever deeper into the surrounding forests to find it. The farther they venture from the camps, the higher the risk of rape. The stoves help women use less wood to cook, lessening their need to gather firewood and be exposed to rape.

The nearby Virunga National Park, home to many species of wild animals, has been increasingly hard hit as refugees roam far and wide to find wood for charcoal, cutting down stands of timber. Charcoal is easy to make, cheap, and consequently in high demand. The charcoal business is controlled by the Hutu FDLR militia, which has established its control inside the park.

Kahorha is a familiar figure in the camp because of his role with ASAE. We walk the rows of tarp-covered huts in a section of the camp filled with the most recent arrivals, where I hope to learn more about the current situation in the countryside.

"There were many people fighting, so we decided to leave," says Salama Boka, a twenty-year-old woman who came to the camp just one month ago with her two daughters. "They are still there," she says of the soldiers, shaking her head in dismay.

The Rwandan troops that swept through eastern Congo earlier in the year, attacking the Hutu FDLR militia, did little to improve the situation here. As far as Boka is concerned, nothing has changed. It is still the Tutsi CNDP militia, which is now part of the Congolese army, fighting with the Hutu FDLR, just as it has always been. "You think we know why they fight? Do you think we people care?" She shakes her head as children tug at her skirt.

Before she fled, she grew cassava, peanuts, and beans. "We were in the village [when we] saw government soldiers advancing. I ran with one child in my arms." She receives extra food rations for her children. She feels somewhat comforted by the recent arrival of her husband, who went missing in the fighting. He is somewhere in the camp now, "asking people if they had seen me," but they've yet to connect.

This is not the first time she's fled her village for a refugee camp. After spending a year or so in a camp, she had returned to her village, thinking it was safe. "I cannot count all the times they surprise you," she says of the militia fighters who suddenly appear from the bush. "When you go to the fields, and you see people running, you don't have time . . . you just go." The endless fighting forces people to live day to day, she complains. "At the market, people only buy what they can carry."

When I press her about why the militias are always fighting, she offers, "I think people are fighting because of hatred." She doesn't mention minerals or mines.

Would she go back?

She shrugs. "I don't know when I can go back. It's not quiet yet. Some people have [recently] died."

When I ask about camp life, Boka points to a nearby concrete pad set up for water and washing. Beyond the concrete is a section occupied by ethnic Pygmies, who like the others have fled the violence for the safety of the Goma refugee camps. The Pygmies are taking her and her neighbor's water, she complains, and insists that the Pygmies have their own water stand.

She gives Kahorha a look of disgust when he says that the water is there for everyone to share. Boka's attitude typifies the deeply seated ethnic jealousies that permeate the region.

Nearby, Serushago Bahati, thirty-seven, struggles to feed her six children after arriving in the camp just two months earlier. She comes from a village in Masisi that is close to Bibatama, the one I visited. "There were clashes," she says, so she took her children to the town of Rubaya, one of the Masisi region's mineral trading centers. When the situation quieted, she returned home, "but the [Tutsi] CNDP went to fight the [Hutu] FDLR." Accustomed to living in the midst of war, Bahati is no longer frightened to see people shot and killed. "It's normal when people fight. It's normal for people to die."

The Rwandan army's sweep through eastern Congo did nothing to help the situation. Rather, it has made life more difficult, Bahati says. Although the Hutu FDLR fled the advancing Rwandan army, it waited for the situation to quiet down, then returned to its previous positions and began exacting revenge on hapless villagers.

"The FDLR was attacking us and accused us of collaborating with the Rwandan troops," she says. The FDLR forced villagers to show them where the Rwandans had gone and where they were camped so it could counterattack. "They were shooting and looting," she says. "People were afraid. There were more victims."

The national army then attacked the FDLR, and "fighting became more intense," forcing her to leave. The FDLR won't return to Rwanda because the militia is making too much money now in eastern Congo, she says. "There were some mines in the [area]," including a few coltan mines controlled by the FDLR. Despite the fighting and the presence of the national army, "they haven't left," she says of the FDLR. "There are still clashes."

Would she go back to her village any time soon?

"It will be the day peace is restored," Bahati says. "As long as there is fighting, it is difficult."

Claude Fashimana is a twenty-seven-year-old refugee from the village of Ruki who fled the fighting in the Masisi district some four months earlier, a victim of the Hutu FDLR fighters who sought revenge after the Rwandan army swept through the region. Hutus accused him and others in his village of collaborating with the Tutsi CNDP, he says, which was based nearby. "People were hunted day and night" by the FDLR fighters. "I decided to leave."

Fashimana is puzzled about the intense clashes around his village, since there are no mines nearby. "We don't understand why they were fighting in this village" because "in other places there was cassiterite, but not in [his village]." His family scattered at the sound of gunfire, and he's not seen them since.

Does he want to go back home?

He shakes his head. "Unless peace is restored, we cannot go home."

Esther Murikatete, thirty-six, is caring for six children and has scars to show for the endless fighting. She pulls at the neck of her knit blouse to show me where she was shot in the shoulder. Murikatete came from the Walikale region two months earlier after frequent moves with her children to escape the bloodshed. "There are fights every day" because the Hutu FDLR controls her village. "They were running [her village]," and not far away was the Tutsi CNDP militia. "All the time they had to fight. [If] they meet you, they beat you. They beat me on the head. They took a machete to my foot."

It's "the problem of hatred," Murikatete explains. "None of them like the other."

There's more to it, I suggest, but she makes it clear that she prefers to ignore this reality.

"I always hear that in our area there are mines in our rivers. But I'm not interested in this." Farming offers little reason for fighting. "Our land is very fertile," and in peaceful times, she grows beans, cassava, and bananas. She longs to return. "I love my village. If today I hear there is no more sound of guns, I will decide to go back home. Here we are starving."

When Murikatete first arrived in the refugee camp, she came with two of her children; then four more came, who are out gathering firewood as we speak. Her children make a little money selling firewood, and they supplement their diet with the produce of a small garden she cultivates on a plot of unclaimed land not far from the camp. Her children also do chores to earn money, such as carrying food or supplies for others. "This is shocking us," she says of camp life. "I wish the authorities could find a solution so we can go back home. Our conditions are very sad."

Widows of Rutshuru

The town of Rutshuru is northwest of Goma in the heart of territory bitterly fought over by the former Tutsi CNDP and the Hutu FDLR. It is a fertile region on the western edge of the sprawling Virunga National Park, home to a wide variety of wildlife, including the endangered mountain gorillas. Kahorha's nonprofit provides seeds to ten women who make up the Rutshuru Widows Association.

It's a deceptively simple project. The seeds provide the women with life-sustaining food, but they're also able to grow enough food to sell for money to build mud-brick homes with metal roofs, along with some latrines. The women have built ten houses, one for each of the association's members.

The seeds are a loan. The association pays back what they've borrowed each growing season in seeds, with interest. So far, the widows have returned about twenty-six pounds of seed as repayment for the twenty pounds they've been given. They take the excess seeds for additional crops, for future sales, or for reserve.

The widows have struggled, however, after taking in others who have fled the fighting. When ASAF learned of their dire situation, Kahorha explains, the group came up with the idea of seeds. The widows needed to grow food, and lots of it, not just once, but year after year.

Helping the women to eventually build better, more secure homes helped them fight the rape epidemic, Kahorha says. Rather than helping victims after rapes had occurred, which is already being done by local clinics, ASAF wanted to get ahead of the problem. "We didn't want to work on the consequences. We work in the community to prevent it, [because] the problem will continue if nothing is done, even though the war is gone."

Many of those who fled the countryside for Rutshuru came from just fifteen or twenty miles away. Though some have returned during a lull in the fighting, the situation remains far from settled. Just a few days earlier, a woman was killed in Rutshuru by armed men, Kahorha says. The circumstances of the killing are unclear, so we have to stay alert, he says, throughout our visit.

We turn off the paved road through Rutshuru and onto a dirt side street, stopping at a modest complex of low, mud-brick buildings at the back of an expanse of neatly swept dirt. I am greeted by the association members led by an elderly woman with smiling eyes. Because of the fighting, most of these women, who have themselves been displaced, have hosted as many as four, five, or more people in their homes. It hasn't been easy. "We suffered for having welcomed [displaced people] in this area," says Maria Bazirake, association president. The women diligently cultivate their gardens, she explains, but hungry refugees uprooted their plants and stole their crops. "It was a difficult period for us," she says of the past couple of years, because after the refugees returned to their villages, the widows were left with nothing.

The women have replanted their crops and are now harvesting, but they still fear the shiftless soldiers from the military units that are supposed to protect them. "Soldiers are taking food now from the women," Bazirake complains. She wants the government to confine the soldiers to their barracks and to pay them so they don't prey on civilians.

"The seeds were very helpful," says Florida Masika. "They helped in getting food for us and our children. It also helps our neighbors who also had no seeds." The problem, she says, is "instability in the region. You have to run away and when you return, you find everything has been taken. We were a small group at first, but after the first harvest, twice as many people helped." The group has harvested crops twice this year and is looking forward to their third harvest in a few months' time.

The seeds have helped the women become self-reliant, says Leocaldie Mutuzo, one of the group's leaders. "We're discriminated against as widows." When a husband dies, families often reject the widow, fearing that she may try to take food and land from the husband's family. "You cannot approach us," the husband's family will say. The widow often is forced to pay rent to the husband's family for a garden plot, pay a portion of the crops she grows, or work a couple of days on the family's land.

The houses the women have built have become the envy of the Rutshuru community. Already skilled growers, they've also become master builders. "We can learn," Mutuzo says proudly. "[We] are developing the area. [We] are making [mud] blocks. Others are [copying] the style."

Senior among the widows is Marie Bizigati, seventy-three, survivor of a lifetime of violence. "The war affected us a lot," she says in a calm and even voice, steeped in understatement. "We lost our children. All the time, we have to run away. We became poorer and poorer."

What is behind all the fighting?

"It is a problem of occupation and wealth," Bizigati says. "The country is providing lots of minerals." But she's not interested in rocks; she much prefers plants and animals. "Our land is very fertile," and there is room for cattle, which is where the community should focus. Although a tentative calm has settled over the region, she thinks it won't last. "The surface fight is over, but the deeper fight is still here and still making us afraid. People are still being taken out of their homes and being killed."

That deeper fight is over the area's minerals, Bizigati says, and the current calm endures only because Congolese national forces are present. But the Hutu FDLR militia hides during the day and comes out under the cover of darkness. "At night, [the villagers are] assaulted by armed men. Some go out for a walk and don't come home. This is the reality." One of her neighbors lost her twenty-two-year-old son several days earlier when he went out at night. "If [soldiers] can find you, they shoot you."

Bizigati echoes the oft-repeated complaint that Congolese army soldiers are as bad as the Hutu FDLR. A lot of the area's problems would be solved if the government soldiers were confined to barracks and paid. Because neither happens, the soldiers attack local residents, loot, and sometimes kill. The community would be better off "if they could make operations against the FDLR," she says. The community is confused over who is fighting whom, since all of the fighters wear similar uniforms. "We don't know who attacks us." The international community could help by stopping the flow of weapons. "They should control the spread of weapons."

The women need corrugated metal sheets for roofing so they can finish their houses. "If we can get them, we can develop," Bizigati says. "We also want a grain storage [facility] so that when the price goes up after the harvest, we can get more money."

At the Gates of the UN

The United Nations' military post outside of Rutshuru is an oasis of orderliness staffed by Indian troops. The camp commanders are off post when Kahorha and I visit, but we meet with an officer who does not want to be identified or quoted, though he talks at length about the UN's mission. The UN tactics are quite familiar and involve placing peacekeepers between combatants to keep them from shooting each other. The idea is that the fighters won't shoot UN soldiers.

It usually works, but not always. I'm hard pressed to find an alternative. Peace in eastern Congo is ultimately up to the Congolese, of course. If the UN peacekeepers engage in hostilities, they become just another army in the midst of mayhem, making themselves more vulnerable to attack than they already are. It is not a position the UN wants to be in, and it is not the UN's role to squash or eliminate opposing forces. Their role is to instill calm so that communities can create their own peace. If the Congolese are unwilling or unable, there's little foreign troops can do.

An unofficial community of refugees spreads from the gates of the UN post, and though I want to talk with them, Kahorha warns that we shouldn't linger. As a *muzungu*, I'm always a target. But, more important, it's late in the day, and this is when people get quite drunk on the locally brewed beer and alcohol distilled in the camp. No sooner does he caution me than a half-dressed, drunken woman staggers up to me, bellowing a demand for money. We slip away and turn our attention to a woman cooking food in front of her tarp-covered hut.

Her name is Maria Maniraguha, a forty-eight-year-old mother of five, who for the past two years has been running from one refugee camp to another. "People came at night. They looted us. It was not possible to live in those conditions." She doesn't know who's to blame for the fighting, only that all soldiers have uniforms. She can't tell one group from another. When she and her neighbors fled her village, four women died in the forest and her two-year-old child was shot dead. "We are ready to go back, but our houses were destroyed. We are waiting for peace to be restored."

Maniraguha stays in touch with her village and has heard that six of her neighbors were killed recently as they collected firewood, so she's not eager to go back. She makes a little money by cultivating other people's gardens. She plans to wait for her next harvest before returning to her village. Maybe then it will be safe.

Mohammed Anasi, a thirty-year-old woman with three children, was forced to leave her home village of Binza, just twenty miles away, because of fighting. She arrived in another refugee camp near Rutshuru in 2006. "Every day there were fights between the [Tutsi] CNDP and the [Hutu] FDLR." She lost three younger brothers to the fighting, two of whom were shot while running away.

She shrugs when I asked what the fighting is about.

"We don't really know. Most were there to loot." She guesses that the Tutsis were attacking the Hutus "to drive them back to [Rwanda]." Integrating the combatants into the national army is not a solution. "The threat is still there" for civilians because the same soldiers are still fighting. "People are still fleeing into the forests" because the Hutu FDLR militia waits for the government forces to leave before it attacks. "If the government forces are there, then the [FDLR] leaves, then comes back."

Anasi is convinced that the FDLR must be removed from eastern Congo. "The solution is to take out the FDLR so we can go back home."

At the very least, she says, the two armies should attempt to settle their differences. "We think they should sit together and discuss, but if they don't want to leave, we can give them land." If the FDLR wants to settle down and live peacefully, it is possible. "When we are told peace is restored, we're ready to go home." She's weary of life in the refugee camps because people are always hungry and the shelters are inadequate. "Children get wet in the rains."

Dangerous Patrols

On the way back to Rutshuru, we meet with community activist Immaculee Sifa, twenty-nine, a recently widowed mother of two children who lives in a modest house just off the main road. She wears neatly pressed jeans and a monogrammed polo shirt. The Hutu FDLR militia has been roaming the area in recent days, she says, and attacked one of her neighbors just a couple of nights earlier. That the FDLR is lurking nearby makes Kahorha anxious, and as I talk with Sifa, he nervously eyes the road traffic.

"Since 1994, there has been no peace here," Sifa says. That was when the Hutus fled Rwanda after the genocide. When the Rwandan Tutsi army invaded in 1996, the Hutus hid weapons in the forests and in the UN's refugee camps. More than a dozen years on, the Hutus are still a menace. "Since 1996 they have been looting." The Hutu militias are killing the nearby park's wildlife, decimating herds of water buffalo, hippos, elephants, and antelope, selling the meat it doesn't eat.

The militias have caused trouble for residents who want to cultivate garden plots, Sifa explains. "Anyone who went to the fields had to pay three bowls of beans." After that is paid, then the farmers "could sell [the rest] and keep the money." In some cases, the militia has forced people to work for them instead of demanding a portion of the produce. The militias might also advance money to a farmer to grow a garden, then claim part of the harvest as repayment. If the farmer doesn't cooperate, it means a gruesome death. "They would find you."

The Hutu militias often demand salt, corn, and other supplies. "They would come and kill. We lost so many people that way."

It's been quiet for the past couple of months because the FDLR has retreated. But "they're still not far from here. They are mixed up with some local men." The Hutus have formed alliances in the community, and together they commit crimes. Just a couple of days earlier, "the house in back of me was attacked by soldiers. Some were outside my door. They looted my neighbor's house. A girl shouted and cried. She knew who was looting." One of the residents, a young man, was shot as he ran away, most likely the same killing the Rutshuru widows told me about.

Those responsible for the attack may be the same soldiers posted by the government to protect the community, Sifa says. Soldiers loot homes while they're supposed to be making security patrols, and they kill anyone who resists. The same soldiers then return to the scene and blame the crime on the Hutu FDLR militia. This is what happened at the house behind her. "People who are here say it was government soldiers" who robbed the house and killed the young man. "Soldiers are not happy" because "they say they don't get their salaries."

Sifa's husband was killed recently along with two others, all supposedly murdered by the Hutu militia. "They say it was the FDLR who killed them." But she doesn't know for sure. She knows only that the violence never ends.

13

CHARCOAL, WILDLIFE, AND ANGRY MAI-MAI

KAHORHA AND I park by the side of the road, little more than two tire tracks chewed out of the lava, at the border of the Virunga National Park just north of Goma. People stream by, some walking, some on bicycles, each carrying at least one bulging bag of charcoal. They've been hoisted overhead, strapped across backs, or piled atop bicycles that the owners struggle to keep upright. Women balance the bags on their heads with babies tied to their backs.

They pause beside an armed soldier who stands twenty yards away and dutifully lower a bag, untie the strings, and add a couple of hand-fuls of charcoal to the growing pile at the soldier's feet. It's their tax, their right to pass, and free income for the soldier, who is guarding the forest against such plunder. Sometimes the charcoal carriers just pay money and move on.

The deforestation of the Virunga National Park has decimated herds of water buffalo, elephants, and hippos and soon could do the same to the critical habitat of the endangered mountain gorilla. It is one of the unseen effects of the fight over minerals in eastern Congo that ripples across the entire region. In one direction, about seventy thousand people struggle to survive in refugee camps, all for the sake of a trickle of metallic ore that might be used in mobile phones or some other high-tech gadget. In the other direction, masses of Africa's magnificent wildlife march toward the precipice of extinction.

The thriving charcoal business is largely controlled by members of the Hutu FDLR who have been chased from their mineral enclaves in eastern Congo into this park. Stripped of the incomes they once derived from coltan and tin mines, the Hutus have captured the forest charcoal industry. But the Hutus don't make the charcoal. They charge a fee or take tribute in the form of food and supplies for that right.

"Most of the [charcoal making] population is from the [refugee] camps," explains Henry Cirhuza, the Congolese program manager for the Gorilla Organization, a London-based nonprofit group working to preserve Africa's mountain gorillas. A ten-year veteran of the organization, Cirhuza specializes in the interface between gorillas and people. "The [national parks] tried to . . . destroy the charcoal operations," he says, but couldn't. Charcoal production is extremely widespread because of the high demand. It's by far the preferred cooking fuel. "Some of the big hotels use charcoal. It's a big challenge."

Efforts to push people to use alternative fuels have also failed. The Congolese army controls access to the forest and the Hutu FDLR controls the interior. Cirhuza says people are sympathetic to the soldiers because "they have to survive" just like everyone else. Instead of protecting the park, however, they're profiting from the charcoal it produces. "Soldiers control access to production areas," he says. "People go into the park with sugar and salt," which is then delivered to the militia fighters in the interior.

So far, Cirhuza maintains, "the gorillas are not affected by the charcoal production. But once [people] cut all the forests, they will move [into gorilla habitat] and the gorilla will be affected." Charcoal production has already destroyed the park's elephant and water buffalo habitat. When soldiers or militias encounter these giant creatures, they kill and butcher them and sell the meat in Goma. Despite the damage to the wildlife, Cirhuza understands the plight of the refugees. "They are starving in the camps," and making charcoal is "an opportunity for them to make some money."

Cirhuza sees little chance the situation will change. Since the camps are located at the park's edge, the refugees profit from the endless demand for charcoal. Coupled with the fact that the camps offer the refugees clean water, toilets, food, and education for their children, he does not expect the camps to empty quickly, even if a permanent peace can be established.

Back at the park's border, Kahorha and I plunge deeper into the forest. We pass at least a dozen more charcoal carriers, and twenty minutes later we pull up at the small village of Rusayo. A half-dozen children play near the road, kicking a soccer ball made of rags. We stop to talk. The oldest of the group says yes, everyone in the village makes charcoal. A big sack sells for about thirty-five dollars, and most of their customers are from the refugee camps or the town, who sell it in town at a higher price.

It's not easy work, the teenager says, declining to give his name. The boys head into the park early, walking at least five or six hours, stopping to take a rest at midday. When they find a good location, they make an agreement with the militia soldiers controlling the area. The boys then chop down trees, pile them in a shallow pit, and cover them with dirt. They set the wood on fire, and, smothered of oxygen, it smolders slowly, until the wood pulp becomes charcoal. The process takes several days, forcing the youngsters to spend nights in the forest sleeping on the ground. Once the smoldering ends and the fire cools, the boys uncover the charcoal, break it into small chunks, bag it, and carry it out. The white plastic gunny sacks are stacked beside the house and sold.

Most of the villagers work one way or another in the charcoal business. All of the money the boys earn is spent on food or other items, because it's too dangerous to save. "If we keep the money, people come to steal the money. If people know you have money, you will be attacked."

Such was the fate of the last adult who lived in the house that the children now occupy. The father was shot after he built the house with the money he had earned from charcoal. The man's wife was poisoned, the boy says, and she left three orphans for whom he is caring.

The teenager thinks he is sixteen or seventeen years old, but he isn't sure. As we speak, he assures me he wants to do more with his life than make charcoal. But at the moment, he has no other choices. "Until I get a new job, I have to look after these kids by making charcoal."

A Question of Survival

An hour later, Kahorha and I navigate rows of white, tarp-covered shelters in the sprawling Mugunga 1 refugee camp, one of the closest to the national park and home to hundreds of charcoal makers. This is a largely Hutu refugee camp, Kahorha explains, which is why Ndegeya Ndamukunzi tells me he has little trouble from the Hutu FDLR militia that controls the park's interior.

"How else can I survive if I don't go into the forest?" Ndamukunzi asks, after settling onto a rock near his family's hut. "They give us one plate of beans a day."

Ndamukunzi has just returned from the forest carrying a gigantic bundle of sticks on his back, the largest an inch or two thick, which he has dropped with a heavy crash. The bundle is worth about two hundred Congolese francs, or about twenty-five US cents, just enough to buy a sack of potatoes. "My children will eat for one day," he says. "That's how we live here." Ndamukunzi has been making charcoal for two years. "Before I didn't make charcoal, I was hungry. Since there is hunger, I learned to make charcoal." It was easy and he learned by following others into the park.

"It's a long way to the forest. Five hours each way," which means he has to spend a night or two there. He often collects firewood that he sells at the camp, but not before cutting down a few trees and starting a charcoal pit fire before he leaves. A couple of days later, he goes back into the park to collect the charcoal.

Access to the prime charcoal areas of the forests has a price. "Before I get access to the park, I have to pay ten dollars to the guards who protect the park." If he has no money, he gives the guards some charcoal. Sometimes Ndamukunzi hires his neighbors as carriers. "Women try to help me, to carry the charcoal. It helps me a lot to get food. I have to get more to eat."

Do the Hutu FDLR militia or the animals cause problems?

Ndamukunzi dismisses the concern with a wave of his hand, somewhat fatalistically. "I'm not afraid to stay in the forest. To stay in the camp is to die, or to go is to die. I have to get something to eat." The fact that there have been clashes between government forces and the FDLR has little significance. "I don't care if one meets me and kills me," he says of the militia fighters. "It's better than to die of hunger." The FDLR has not been a problem. "I never met them. I'm more afraid of the [Tutsi] CNDP."

Ndamukunzi, forty-four, has ten children. His oldest son, twenty-three, recently married and joined him in the charcoal-making business. The marriage did not follow protocol, because his son was unable to pay the bride price. But the girl's family let her get married with the understanding that the son would pay the money from his charcoal profits.

Ndamukunzi dismisses the fact that charcoal threatens the park's wildlife, including the endangered mountain gorillas. "Animals and human beings are not equal," he says. It is unfortunate that the animals are killed, but he makes charcoal to survive. He would quit what he does, however, "if they take us back home."

Ndamukunzi is from the village of Karuba, a place I visited on the trip to the Masisi coltan mine, a community known for its cows and the milk they produce. We stopped at the village on our return trip and Kahorha and the others purchased containers of fresh milk. But Ndamukunzi has no plans to return. "I have no house. It was destroyed. My land was taken. I don't know how [I can] survive." The land he once tilled "is used for cows." The Tutsi CNDP drove the Hutus from the village, he says, and took his land. "Staying here or going home is the same," because prospects are equally grim in both places. If he returned to his village, "I would have to work for other people." But in this camp he's self-employed.

Wouldn't the village be better than living in the crowded, desperate conditions of the refugee camp?

He shakes his head, saying that the Masisi region is still violent. "If I am told all is OK, I can go back home." But it is still not safe, he insists. "There are people who were killed individually. Killed by some people."

Who and why?

Ndamukunzi shrugs. "I'm not a politician. I don't know why they're fighting. We could only see them shooting."

Hope for Hippos

The World Wildlife Federation is among several international organizations struggling to stave off disaster for the region's wild animals at the hands of poachers and the growing cadre of charcoal makers. In a quiet compound in a corner of Goma I find Thierry Bodson, the program manager for the WWF.

Can the destruction of the surrounding forests be stopped?

He shakes his head wearily. Fighting in the region has forced many people into Goma, which now is a city of about six hundred thousand people. But the town's infrastructure can accommodate only about fifty thousand people. "Instability has brought many [refugees] to Goma. They have stayed for their own safety." Having five-hundred-thousand-plus people in and around the city has created a demand for land, food, and fuel that is decimating the environment. More than 95 percent of the population uses charcoal. "In the city of Goma, they use charcoal. The only way to provide energy is wood, unfortunately."

Virunga National Park is so big that "the park is a good place to hide. It's easy," which is why the Hutu FDLR militia is there. And "you have a lot of animals," which provide meat. "A lot of people have guns," and consequently "the government is unable to tackle the problem."

Also, Bodson says, it is "difficult to control the [government] soldiers. They are killing animals as well. With a gun you can kill a lot of animals." It "takes a lot of forest" to sustain the charcoal business. The park has that forest, and it is very accessible, so a lot of people are involved. "Charcoal is a very lucrative business."

The WWF is trying to cut the dependency on charcoal. "If you can reduce the consumption by 50 percent, it makes a big difference," Bodson tells me. So the organization is "investing in people to plant trees." Another tactic they have tried is introducing briquettes made of compressed and dried vegetable matter. I've seen the round, doughnut-shaped briquettes in several places in Goma. The briquettes are cheap and easy to make and burn well, so Bodson is optimistic. "It's a way to save trees as much as possible." But the briquettes have yet to catch on.

Turning the tide against the charcoal makers is tough, Bodson sighs. "It's like a war" inside the park. "They are very dangerous people," he says of FDLR. "Last week a ranger was killed." For the short term, "the mountain gorillas are well protected" because of international support and attention.

But the rest of the wildlife is being decimated. "If you attack a hippo, it is not news." The hippo population that once thrived at the edge of Lake Kivu is dwindling. This in turn affects fish species that feed on hippo excrement in the lake's shallows. The water buffalo population has dropped from about 23,000 in 1959 to just 3,800 in 2006, the last time a census was done. Elephants numbered 2,800 in 1959, but only 348 were left in 2006, Bodson tells me.

Malaise of the Mai-Mai

Along with the region's environment and wildlife, indigenous communities have been devastated by mayhem in eastern Congo. These ethnic Congolese communities have formed militias known as the Mai-Mai, which are often as active as the other armed groups though frequently overlooked in the chaos. The Mai-Mai revere the spirit world and practice witchcraft. They habitually wear charms and amulets and use herbs, potions, and oils, convinced these protect them from bullets. The Mai-Mai have drawn criticism from human rights groups for their use of child soldiers, who are easily indoctrinated into the militias and their magical practices.

Didier Bitaki, thirty-six, a lawyer and the son of a regional leader, does not represent the fearsome Mai-Mai warriors, who are often photographed wearing white face paint and branches tied to their arms and legs. He's been a commander with the Mai-Mai and took part in the negotiations that ended fighting in eastern Congo in 2003, yet he sports a dark gray shirt and matching pants and looks distinctly clean-cut. During the time he served, the Mai-Mai were brought into the national army and he was made a colonel. He resigned, however, for a chance to live and study in Japan, where he stayed for five years before returning to the Congo.

The Mai-Mai make up the fourth group of combatants in eastern Congo and are often involved in the fighting between the Tutsi and Hutu militias as well as the Congolese army. Bitaki believes that economic struggles, in which the mines and minerals of the region play a part, are at the root of the fighting in eastern Congo. The Mai-Mai are the most disenfranchised group in eastern Congo, ignored by both current president Joseph Kabila and his late father, Laurent Kabila, whom the Mai-Mai had helped put into power. Bitaki tells me that the Congolese government has "forgotten those who supported them. We contributed a lot to bringing change to the country."

The Mai-Mai are dismayed by the exploitation of minerals and the money being made in the midst of fighting and chaos. "It's those who come from outside who show the Congolese how to exploit the minerals. The problem is not based on minerals. Most armed groups exploiting minerals have links to powers outside the country. Minerals are not the source [of violence], but [violence] is one of the consequences [of mining]."

"Frustrations are forcing people to take up weapons," says Bitaki. The Kabila government "made agreements to take [the Mai-Mai] and use us in different institutions in the country." But it has not happened. "We are not well represented."

Bitaki believes that involving the Mai-Mai in the government will lessen the need for armed confrontation. The Mai-Mai are forced to fight because the government refuses to include them. "Why did

[we] become armed groups? The main responsibility [rests] with the government." The Mai-Mai have not given up, however. "We are still discussing things with the government." But if the government fails to respond, "maybe we go back to the bush and start fighting. The government is trying to solve everything by force," having realized too late that it needs to take control of eastern Congo in order to save it from destruction. Bitaki says that the Mai-Mai want peace but also demand a position in the regional government. If the government continues to shun them, "maybe we will [again] become rebels against the government."

Following the 1994 genocide in Rwanda, the Hutu *interahamwe* militias swarmed into eastern Congo. The government armed the Mai-Mai to defend their communities. But the Mai-Mai soon realized they had become pawns in a larger game. Because the Congolese army alone could not resist Rwanda and Uganda's second invasion in 1998, Kabila armed the Hutu FDLR militia to help fight. The Mai-Mai were caught in the middle.

"We were obliged to get into the conflict because our people were being killed every day." The Mai-Mai were trained and armed by the FDLR, he says, with the intention of helping the Hutus fight the Rwandan Tutsis, and they suffered the consequences.

"We are asking the government to protect civilians now. We want them to integrate some Mai-Mai leaders [into government]. If they don't do that, the Mai-Mai will stay in the bush."

Don't the Mai-Mai also exploit the region's minerals?

Bitaki shakes his head, saying that the Mai-Mai don't because mining has destabilized the region. "Show me the name of a Mai-Mai commander" who is doing that. "I've never been connected or implicated in any wrong. We are [only] exploiting our land" to grow crops and raise animals. "We are citizens. It is our citizens who are protecting [the land] and who are supported by the people."

The Mai-Mai have a strong sense of community, unlike the Hutu or the Tutsis from Rwanda. "I work for my people. If we copy what others are doing to this country, we will never build this country."

Exploitation is to blame for the demise of eastern Congo. "Those who are looting the country, let them go ahead." The Mai-Mai will never exploit minerals. "We cannot encourage [that]. It's better for me to stay with the poor people." Mai-Mai prefer a life of "making agriculture and simple business."

"[Mai-Mai] have been used," Bitaki says, but the government is "not taking care of [us]. That's why this government is not credible. We will continue to resist."

I point out that the government, in fact, has responded to the Mai-Mai complaints, but won't make any Mai-Mai appointments as long as the Mai-Mai threaten war.

Bitaki says the government's response is nonsense. "Most [political] leaders come from rebel movements" and have disarmed in exchange for government posts. It's standard procedure. But once in power, he complains, they do little to help their communities. "What change did they bring to the country? Nothing."

In contrast, the Mai-Mai are "ready to fight for liberty and freedom," and "they reject what is being done to them" by the exploitation of minerals.

The Mai-Mai hope to evolve into a political party to legitimize their claim to government positions. Once politically organized, says Bitaki, the Mai-Mai will support political candidates, but at the moment "we don't have the means for that." The Mai-Mai recognize that "staying in the bush and buying weapons is not a solution. Maybe we can find change through democratic ways."

The Mai-Mai remain angry, however, because "people in Kinshasa [are] only for themselves." For example, teachers in the region often go unpaid while members of parliament earn thousands of dollars per month. The government collects taxes and fees, but people never see the benefits. "The money [does] not reach the people. That is why we call [government officials] the enemies of the country." Most public employees are not paid, forcing them to demand bribes. "The government is creating the corruption" in the midst of the region's mineral wealth. "Those who confiscate the wealth have confiscated the government. How can the country move ahead?" If the Mai-Mai are in government, he says, "we will see some change."

Islands in the Stream

Keeping up with the refugee problem is one of the unforgiving tasks performed by the UN High Commission on Refugees, which maintains a large office in Goma. Here I meet with a UNHCR official who is eager to discuss the situation in eastern Congo but can only do so anonymously, due to the sensitive role played by the UN. A veteran of several years in the region and multiple assignments in some of the world's worst disaster zones, he offers insight into the killing fields of the Congo.

The official tells me that it's difficult to pinpoint a sole cause or solution to the conflicts in eastern Congo because "there is no central part of what is happening . . . so you can't say: this is the problem."

Some causes are obvious, such as the lack of a central government, I reply.

He agrees but suggests that a stronger central government might not solve anything since "some in government are part of the problem." Giving such people more power would only make things worse. The national capital, Kinshasa, is very far from Goma, so "how much influence could it have?" With no central control, "who has control over what resources?"

Most local governments "operate by and for themselves," and since they're relatively weak, this helps both the Congolese army and the militias. "They use the exploitation of minerals to arm and equip themselves." The Hutu FDLR is deceptively effective in the field, he says. "They have informal structures," but "they are very well organized."

When the Tutsi CNDP militia took over the region after the Ugandan and Rwandese forces withdrew in 2003, it took land from locals and put its own people in charge, the official tells me. Many of the non-Tutsi villagers were forced to flee, and now they fill the refugee camps in Goma, confirming what the charcoal maker told me. Though most refugees want to return to their villages, "they do not want to face these people," who are the same ones who took their land. "How do they go back home? Their land has been taken. Their land is occupied."

The Congolese government has not solved any problems by incorporating the Tutsi CNDP into the national army, since these same units still occupy the same territory as before, now under the guise of the government. Nearly two million people are displaced in the region, he says. The UN has six refugee camps that contain about seventy thousand people displaced from the Masisi and Rutshuru areas, and more camps are being set up. But the camps hold only a small portion of the refugees, because the vast majority are scattered around the Goma region, living with friends and family.

The UN wants the refugees to return to their villages, but they can't because their land has been taken. In the fighting over the years, schools and hospitals have been destroyed, yet another disincentive to vacate the camps, where food, education, and health care are provided.

This official says that killing and rape continue in the countryside. The Hutu FDLR militia has to be removed. That was supposed to happen when the government allowed the Rwandan army to sweep through the region in early 2009, but it did nothing to resolve the situation for the Mai-Mai, who wished to establish command and control over the wanton Congolese army.

Although the UN's nearly twenty thousand soldiers in the Congo represent the largest UN force in the world, that force "is nothing" compared to the size of the country or the scope of the peacekeeping problem.

I ask what more the UN can do.

If the UN is guilty of anything, the official responds, "we are responsible for not speaking out enough."

Major external forces at work in eastern Congo are international corporations, he continues. "They are a major source of power in the region. The international corporate world is deeply involved in what is going on here." They provide the impetus for miners to dig the valuable ore and for militias to fight over the mines and the money they earn.

International corporations, via their dealers, inject huge amounts of cash into the country. That cash keeps the situation churning.

Serious questions need to be asked and answered, he concludes. "How committed is the international community to ending the conflict? What have [international corporations] been doing to stop the conflict when they are in the country exploiting minerals?" If the situation in eastern Congo is to be solved, it can only be done "if the countries put pressure on the companies to tell us where the minerals come from."

It may be that pressure is already on the way.

14

THINGS FALL APART

WITH LAURENT Nkunda's former CNDP rebels reveling in their status as members of the Congolese army, by late 2009 they have tightened their grip on the eastern Congo's lucrative tin and coltan mines. They operate what could be called a mafia-style extortion racket: the Tutsi soldiers tax villagers for the right to break rocks, and they rake in more money than they ever dreamed possible. "Last year's high profile offensives against the [Hutu militia] FDLR paved the way for high-ranking elements of the ex-CNDP to gain and consolidate access to mineral wealth," grumbled Global Witness activist Annie Dunnebacke, freshly back to the London drizzle after a month in eastern Congo. "Control of the mines has effectively been transferred from one group of armed thugs to another—the main difference being that the new ones are wearing the national army's uniform."[1]

Chances that the situation in eastern Congo might change are slim. "For more than a decade now, the country's mineral wealth has provided an incentive and a cash base for the conflict to continue," Dunnebacke said. "Unless the government and international donors implement a comprehensive strategy which tackles once and for all the economic drivers of this conflict, the local population will continue to suffer and the country's future will continue to be blighted."[2]

According to Dunnebacke, the strategy of the Congolese government for the misty hills of Masisi is clear, and with it comes the tacit agreement of aid groups, the UN, and foreign governments. Equilibrium has been attempted; wrapping the strongest force in the region into the national army has stopped some of the worst abuses. The former CNDP and Hutu FDLR have staked out their territories, and as long as each stays put, calm drifts in the air. And if the situation persists, Congolese officials hope, the pesky human rights campaigners might go home, leaving the captains of conflict minerals to plunder in peace.

But risks remain. With very little provocation, eastern Congo could easily revert to savagery that has become as familiar as an old pair of shoes. "The capacity of the former rebels to siphon off revenue from the mines means they could afford to re-arm if they decide peace no longer suits them," said Global Witness activist Emilie Serralta. "This is particularly dangerous considering the ex-commanders' history of reverting to rebellion when they don't get what they want."[3]

Pressure has continued to mount, meanwhile, for international companies and the people they deal with to better track sources of minerals so that conflict minerals are kept off the market. "It's not enough for companies to rely on promises made or paperwork filled out by their suppliers," Dunnebacke said. "If companies want to avoid being complicit in the conflict and human rights abuses, they have to carry out investigations to find out exactly which mines the goods come from, and who has benefited from the trade." It takes very little effort, because "information about who controls which mine site is common knowledge in the trading towns of eastern Congo. Companies buying minerals from militarized areas have no excuse for claiming ignorance."[4]

Yet as pressure grows for more to be done in eastern Congo to stem the violence and choke off the flow of conflict minerals, the United Nations seems to be moving in the opposite direction. Flying in the face of common sense and against calls from activists familiar with eastern Congo, in 2009 the UN caved in to demands from the

Congolese government that the twenty-thousand-plus peacekeepers should go home. The officials suggested that although the Kivu provinces remain restive, the rest of the country has no more need for the UN. The Security Council later modified the drawdown decision, but as with most issues in the region, the future remains unpredictable.

Any decrease in UN troops in the Congo frightens many. Global Witness wants more, not less, UN involvement. The UN should monitor the mineral trail as an impartial observer by being "given the authorization and the means, not only to monitor and inspect mineral shipments, but also support efforts to curtail illegal activities involving the military."[5]

Surprise Arrests

In late 2009, as eastern Congo drifted into uncertain seas, the German government created an international stir by arresting the two top leaders of the Hutu FDLR militia. Both men had been directing FDLR operations in eastern Congo from their homes in Germany, some four thousand miles away. On November 17, 2009, in southern Germany, German federal officers grabbed Ignace Murwanashyaka, the forty-six-year-old leader of the FDLR, and his deputy, Straton Musoni, forty-eight. "The accused are strongly suspected, as members of the foreign terrorist organization FDLR, of committing crimes against humanity and war crimes," the police announced. "FDLR militias are believed to have killed several hundred civilians, raped numerous women, plundered and burned countless villages, forcing villagers from their homes and recruiting numerous children as soldiers."[6]

Though he denied that Hutu militias committed any crimes, Murwanashyaka had been on the UN's radar since 2005, when he was one of fifteen people whose assets were frozen by the UN Security Council on suspicion that he was part of the 1994 Rwandan genocide and then later crimes in eastern Congo. Murwanashyaka had lived in Germany on and off since the late 1980s, after arriving on a study fellowship. He obtained a PhD in economics there, married a German woman, and was given political asylum in 2000. The following year Murwanashy-aka was elected head of the FDLR.

The arrests were a striking reversal from what many say is international indifference to the bloodshed in eastern Congo. Extensive evidence showed that the men had been directing day-to-day operations of the FDLR, to the point of ordering attacks. In their November 2009 report to the UN Security Council, the UN experts wrote that "FDLR leadership in Germany has been in frequent contact with FDLR military officials between September 2008 and August 2009" and documented more than 240 satellite phone calls between Murwanashyaka and FDLR field commanders. In one instance, a March 2009 order issued by a top FDLR commander directed soldiers to "create a humanitarian catastrophe." Such orders were typically made only after consultation with Murwanashyaka.[7]

Experts also reported that he had been critical to raising funds and purchasing supplies with money earned by the FDLR from minerals sales.

> Mr. Murwanashyaka has been involved in managing large sums of money that had been raised through the illicit sale of natural resources derived from areas under the control of FDLR. This money is used by the leadership to pay for operational needs such as the telephone bills of satellite telephones used by the FDLR military high command. Some of these funds, together with others that have been raised externally by the leadership, are then transferred back to FDLR officers in the Democratic Republic of the Congo via bank transfer and through Western Union and other money transfer agencies for uses such as medical treatment for FDLR officers.[8]

One of the biggest mineral trading houses in Bukavu, South Kivu, known as Etablissement Muyeye, regularly moved money to people working closely with Murwanashyaka, the UN experts found. Money transfers totaling tens of thousands of dollars were facilitated by friends and family members used as senders and recipients to avoid the international freeze on the leader's assets.[9]

The arrests took two key players out of the violent mix in eastern Congo, crippling the FDLR for the short term by pulling out its linchpin. "This will certainly weaken the FDLR," said Anneke Van Woudenberg, senior researcher on the Congo for Human Rights Watch. "This will send quite a shock, for Ignace Murwanashyaka to be arrested, because the FDLR very much thought it could go about [its] business in Europe and the U.S. with impunity. [Former FDLR combatants] all say 'we do nothing without the OK of Ignace Murwanashyaka,' so taking him out the picture will have a big effect."[10]

While Germany was commended for its action, two other Western countries harboring accused Hutu militiamen did not act. Callixte Mbarushimana, the secretary general of the FDLR, was residing in France in late 2009; and Jean-Marie Vianney Higiro, the president of the breakaway faction of the FDLR known as the Rally for Unity and Democracy (RUD), was thought to reside in the United States.

"What I like about what happened is that this is the first time, to my knowledge, that the Europeans are arresting the FDLR on the basis of something that is currently happening in Congo, not actions of the genocide in 1994," said Guillaume Lacaille, a senior researcher on the Congo for the International Crisis Group in Nairobi. "This opens up new legal grounds to go after the FDLR. In terms of impact, I would not like to be an FDLR combatant right now." He added, "Now, I would hope that France and the US will follow the example of Germany."[11]

Rwandan officials also praised the arrests. "[The African] Great Lakes region will never know peace if the people leading and raising money for such groups are living freely in Europe and North America," said Tharcisse Karugarama, Rwanda's minister of justice. "It's already high time that the world took decisive action on this issue."[12]

There were no indications from the Obama administration that it intended to act against Higiro, even though bills before Congress demanded steps to curb the violence in eastern Congo arising from conflict minerals. Likewise, UN investigators reported they had received no cooperation or response to appeals for help from officials in the United States, France, Belgium, or other European countries where Hutu FDLR associates were said to live.

(In early January 2011, a French court will rule that Callixte Mbarushimana should be extradited from France and transferred to the custody of the ICC in The Hague so that he can stand trial on charges of war crimes and crimes against humanity, including murder, torture, and rape. The charges will be based on events in eastern Congo during 2009, when his FDLR militia fought with the UN-backed coalition of Congolese and Rwandan forces.)

A Crisis Deepens

The November 2009 arrest of the two Hutu militia leaders came just a week after the UN experts' latest report was handed to the UN Security Council. In it, the experts shone a harsh light on the dim workings of the mineral trade in eastern Congo, a chaotic plunderfest with tentacles that reach around the globe. The report opened the blinds on regional and international networks of players among whom few, if any, show an interest in helping the Congo solve its problems or alleviating its suffering.

> The . . . FDLR's ongoing exploitation of natural resources in the Kivus, notably gold and cassiterite reserves, . . . continues to deliver millions of dollars in direct financing into the FDLR coffers. . . . FDLR gold networks are tightly intertwined with trading networks operating within Uganda and Burundi as well as in the United Arab Emirates. [A] number of mineral exporting companies . . . continue to trade with FDLR [and] end buyers for this cassiterite include the Malaysia Smelting Corporation, and the Thailand Smelting and Refining Company, which is held by Amalgamated Metals Corporation, based in the United Kingdom of Great Britain and Northern Ireland.[13]

The experts' November 2009 report extended and expanded what they wrote in May 2009 debunking the stated purpose of the joint military operation by the Rwandans and Congolese against the Hutu FDLR:

> Scores of villages have been raided and pillaged, thousands of houses have been burnt and several hundred thousand people have been displaced in order to escape from violence generated by military operations. Several hundred people have been killed by [now national army] troops and FDLR reprisal attacks during this period. The operations have also been a vector through which former CNDP officers have cemented their control over mineral-rich areas. . . . Former CNDP units have also forcibly displaced large numbers of civilians from land in . . . Masisi in order to find grazing areas for cattle being brought in from Rwanda.[14]

The Hutu FDLR forces did not scatter after the operation but instead went on a recruiting spree among their ethnic Hutu communities in Burundi and Uganda, said the experts. The future of eastern Congo looked increasingly bleak:

> Military operations have thus not succeeded in neutralizing FDLR, have exacerbated the humanitarian crisis in the Kivus, and have resulted in an expansion of CNDP's military influence in the region. Elsewhere, in Europe, North America and the wider African region, the FDLR diaspora support networks have continued to operate and have been deeply involved in managing the response to the FARDC operations.[15]

It was not an accident that the Kivus continued their slide into chaos, or that little had been done on the ground to diminish the power of the Hutu militias, which had long enjoyed cooperation and support from inside the Congolese government. The UN experts found

at least one critical Hutu link to the upper echelons of the Congolese government in the person of its minister for decentralization and
democracy, Mbusa Nyamwisi. Known widely as just Mbusa, he had
been a key figure in the bloodiest years of the Ituri region, described
in earlier chapters. Mbusa's Hutu link was a man named Kasereka
Maghulu, known as Kavatsi, who operated Galaxy Airlines, a fleet of
cargo planes swooping in and out of eastern Congo.

Kavatsi had a history of working closely with the Hutu FDLR and
Mai-Mai groups that controlled the mines, helping them to obtain
"food supplies and ammunition in return for minerals or timber that
it had exploited or traded." Of particular interest were the gold mines
around Lubero in North Kivu, where Kavatsi "has been involved in
pre-financing gold exploitation in the areas west of Lubero, jointly
controlled by FDLR and Mai Mai Lafontaine elements, in return for
providing general merchandise eventually transported into Butembo
by Galaxy Airlines."[16] Butembo is a gold trading center and key export
point.

Exploitation networks typically cross borders. UN experts found
that neighboring Tanzania, just across Lake Tanganyika, worked as a
natural conduit for arms purchased with Hutu gold that was boated
across the lake. While buying arms, the commanders also recruited.
The experts determined that a key figure in the Tanzanian arms deals
was a long-time resident of the Tanzania capital of Dar es Salaam with
high-level ties to the Congolese government. Those ties were to the
late Congolese president, Laurent-Désiré Kabila, the father of the current president, Joseph Kabila.

Poring over telephone records, UN investigators found frequent
conversations between arms dealers, Tanzanian officials, military
officers, and diplomats, suggesting a network that involved Ugandan
businessmen and a South African man thought to deal in illegal diamonds who traveled frequently to the Congo. Additional leads drew
investigators to Kenya, France, Italy, and the Netherlands. Even reli-
gious groups seemed to be involved, including some Italian citizens
and Catholic missionaries. In one instance, UN investigators said a
Spanish man apparently promised he could raise $200,000 for the

Hutu FDLR from people critical of the Rwandan government for its alleged revenge killings against Hutus following the 1994 Rwandan genocide. Other instances revealed Hutu help was provided by a Belgian priest once posted in Kigoma, a town in Tanzania on the shores of Lake Tanganyika, and a Catholic missionary posted in South Kivu.

Gold to Guns

Most of the Congo's gold is pirated out of the county, according to the Congolese government, totaling forty tons of pure gold per year with an estimated value of $1.4 billion. UN experts estimated that the Hutu FDLR was earning several million dollars a year at least from that illicit gold trade, much of it being moved through Uganda and Burundi to the United Arab Emirates. As previously mentioned, the FDLR controls some of the richest deposits in the Lubero district of North Kivu.

Among the companies dealing in gold from the FDLR-controlled mines was Glory Minerals, which sold gold to a Belgian company, according to UN experts. Glory Minerals told the UN investigators that it didn't deal in Hutu gold, but UN experts insisted otherwise, detailing travel by Glory Minerals associates from eastern Congo to Kampala, Uganda, and on to Dubai, United Arab Emirates, where the gold was sold in perhaps the world's largest gold market.[17]

Despite UN bans on such commercial activity, UN investigators found that two companies, Machanga Ltd. and Uganda Commercial Impex Ltd., were owned by businessmen of Indian origin who "prefinanced" the purchase of gold in eastern Congo and cornered the market. "The gold is then smuggled to Kampala by road or by commercial flight to Entebbe and finally on to Dubai, where it is handled by an associate of both families."[18] This same family associate was an acknowledged supplier of gold to Emirates Gold, a major gold refinery in Dubai, the UN report stated.

While the UN experts believed that about six hundred pounds of gold were moved through Uganda each month, they found other routes for Hutu FDLR gold through neighboring Burundi and through South

Kivu, across Lake Tanganyika, and into Tanzania. In some instances, the gold trade through Burundi was aided by Burundian intelligence officials. "Several sources in Burundi stated that [a key trader] benefits from his relationship with governmental officials in customs and security agencies, including General Adolphe Nshimirimana, the Director General of the Burundian intelligence services," the UN report stated.[19]

The "key trader," identified in the report as Mutoka Ruganyira, appeared to work with many gold dealers in the region as well as communicating regularly with gold traders in Belgium, the experts found. Ironically, Ruganyira's company had been renamed in September 2008 from Gold Link Burundi Trading to Berkenrode BVBA, which happened to be the name of a Belgian gold company that also owned a gold-smelting operation in Antwerp, Belgium. When contacted by the UN, owners of both the Congolese and the Belgian companies told the UN investigators that there was no connection between the two. The Belgian owner, however, also operated a company registered at the Dubai Multi Commodity Center that was known to handle gold.[20]

The Case Against Tin

UN investigators found that the Hutu FDLR controlled cassiterite, coltan, and wolframite mines in eastern Congo that generated several million dollars a year for the militia. A number of companies regularly dealt with known FDLR mine sites during 2009, even as UN experts conducted their probe. One was the Huaying Trading Company (HTC), a Chinese-run *comptoir* based in Goma and Bukavu. Another was Clepad, a Goma-based *comptoir* also thought to be selling tin ore that originated in FDLR-controlled mines in South Kivu. These *comptoirs* were among the key exporters of tin ore from eastern Congo, and they included other members of the Congo's association of mineral dealers, the Enterprise Federation of the Congo. This is the same group whose spokesman, John Kanyoni, I interviewed in August 2009, and which was helping to formulate a disclosure policy aimed at curbing the purchase of conflict minerals.[21]

One of the supply chains followed by the UN investigators involved the sale of minerals purchased by HTC, which had sold minerals to African Ventures Ltd., an entity registered in Samoa but having an address in Hong Kong. The investigators found that African Ventures Ltd. operated as an intermediary for a Swiss businessman named Chris Huber, who had been mentioned by Congolese officials and in other reports as having been involved in the transport of coltan out of the eastern Congo and Rwanda between 1998 and 2003, the most violent period in eastern Congo.

When he was contacted by UN investigators, Huber explained that he was a consultant for African Ventures Ltd. in Hong Kong as well as Refractory Metals Mining Company Ltd. (RMMC), which had an address at Shing Wan Road in Hong Kong, on the same street as African Ventures Ltd. Both companies were thought to have been suppliers to the Thailand Smelting and Refining Company Ltd. (Thaisarco), the company held by Amalgamated Metal Corporation (AMC) of the United Kingdom.[22]

According to the UN report, one of the key people involved with RMMC was John Crawley, also named as a director of a US tantalum processing company, Niotan Inc., based in Nevada. Crawley told UN investigators that he was active in urging greater transparency and accountability in the eastern Congo minerals trade. He wrote the following in an e-mail to the UN investigators:

> As I understand the situation on African Ventures [AVL], the company was set up to [sic] in order to purchase and hold concessions in the [Congo] that would form the basis of our long term mine investment strategy. In the mean time the ITRI [industry association] program was started and AVL then become involved in the purchase of Tin and Tantalum raw materials from other miners in the DRC.
>
> The company collects all transparency documents required by the ITRI transparency program. I am informed that these documents are complete and in good order. AVL also makes

sure that all DRC taxes are paid, all exports comply with the DRC mining code by licensed exporters. Thaisarco ultimately received all of the Tin raw material sourced by this firm, all of the tantalum bearing raw material was sent to Chinese firms. None of the raw material or material produced from the AVL raw material has ever been purchased by Niotan, Inc.

. . . RMMC shipped to Thaisarco in 2009 the following: a. 928 [metric tons] [Congo] origin material. b. 424 [metric tons] Rwanda origin material. c. 423 [metric ton] Nigeria origin.

[African Ventures Ltd.] has supplied RMMC 928 [metric tons] tin ore plus 53 [metric tons] tantalite i.e. all DRC origin minerals.[23]

Clearly sensitive about the references to Niotan in the report, Crawley stated emphatically that Niotan Inc. was not involved in the purchase of tin ore and coltan ore from the Congo. Among other details, however, UN investigators included in their report a piece of company correspondence explaining that until January 2009, RMMC of Hong Kong had been known as Niotan Ltd. The letters says the name had been changed to avoid any confusion between Niotan Ltd. and Niotan Inc., since they were "completely different entities with different shareholders."[24]

If nothing else, the details and documentation uncovered by UN investigators show how extensive and how complex the international networks and relationships are in and around the minerals trade in eastern Congo.

Sensitivities around the issue stem from the United Nations arms embargo that has long been imposed on the Congo. Of course, mining companies and mineral buyers aren't supplying arms. But if the militias use the money that comes from international companies to buy arms, that's a problem. The UN Security Council's Resolution 1807, adopted on March 31, 2008, recognized "the linkage between the illegal exploitation of natural resources, illicit trade in such resources and the proliferation and trafficking of arms as one of the factors fuelling and exacerbating conflicts in the Great Lakes region of Africa." The resolution requires that "all States shall take the necessary measures to prevent the direct or indirect supply, sale or transfer, from their territories or by their nationals . . . of arms and any related materiel, and the provision of any assistance, advice or training related to military activities, including financing and financial . . . assistance, to all non-governmental entities and individuals operating in the territory of the Democratic Republic of the Congo." Loosely interpreted, buying minerals from groups or mines controlled by the FDRL militia or the CNDP militia or any other armed group could be considered providing financial assistance to those groups. In an adroit move to avoid the complexities of the arms embargo, the Congolese government recently wrapped CNDP into the national army.

Help from Helicopters

Government and military profiteering in minerals surfaced as investigators examined the use of a Russian helicopter leased by the Congolese National Police early in 2009. Helicopters are an efficient way to haul arms and supplies into eastern Congo and carry tin and coltan ore out, due to the remote and inaccessible locations of mines. After the Congolese-Rwandan February 2009 offensive against the Hutu FDLR, a number of Rwandan intelligence officers apparently stayed behind to work with the Congolese national army commanders.

But their work appears to have had little to do with security. A white Mi-8 helicopter owned by a Ukrainian company was leased to the Congolese police by Aerospace Consortium, a company from the United Arab Emirates. The leasing documents were signed by John Numbi, head of the Congolese police, who has managed joint military operations with Major General James Kaberebe, the chief of the Rwandan army. In the four months ending in early June 2009, while the helicopter was stationed in Goma, it made forty trips. The flights were listed as local. Aviation sources told investigators that "most of the time the helicopter was used for the peace talks and evacuation of wounded personnel and shifting of Cargo [sic] from DRC to Rwanda and back."[25]

Although the precise routes the helicopter flew could not be determined, the duration of those forty flights raised investigators' suspicions. One flight in late April 2009, for example, lasted four hours. Another at about the same time lasted six hours, though the destination listed was the mineral-rich Masisi district, only a fifteen-minute flight from Goma. Given the proximity of Masisi to Goma and the Rwandan border, it is possible to make multiple trips to Kigali in that time span.

Mismatched Records

Another aspect of the minerals trade between eastern Congo and Rwanda is that import and export records frequently don't match, even when they involve the same entities. Many observers have concluded that few, if any, people, really know how much mineral ore is actually exported from eastern Congo.

UN investigators found that the Goma-based mineral trading company Hill Side filed reports with the Congolese government indicating that in the first four months of 2009, it purchased about 16,500 pounds of tin ore from the Walikale region, where the lucrative Bisie mine is located. Yet aviation records showed that in just two days in April 2009, Hill Side reported that it purchased 11,600 pounds of ore in Walikale, about two-thirds of the total reported for the prior four months. What about the rest of the days, weeks, and months? Was there very little activity in the prior three and a half months?

In another set of statistics obtained by investigators, this time from Rwanda, Hill Side reported that it provided the company Minerals Supply Africa (MSA), a Rwandan company owned by UK businessman David Bensusan, with about 406,500 pounds of ore during that four-month period in 2009—almost twenty-five times what Hill Side officially told the Congolese authorities. Obviously the minerals couldn't have been imported into Rwanda without first being exported from eastern Congo, but Congolese records didn't reflect that. Another set of Congolese figures showed that Hill Side exported about 250,000 pounds of tin ore during the first nine months of 2009, also sending it to MSA. According to internal records for MSA, however, the company imported approximately 800,000 pounds of tin ore from Hill Side for the same period, three times the amount recorded in official Congolese data.

Speaking to UN investigators, Bensusan explained that he "prefinanced" *comptoirs* in Goma, including Hill Side, with money to buy minerals. Bensusan said that roughly 30 percent of what he exported from the region normally came from Rwanda, with about 70 percent coming from eastern Congo. But when UN investigators reviewed official certificates of Bensusan's exports from Rwanda for the period, they found that most of the material reportedly originated in Rwanda.

Certificates showed that the MSA ore was purchased by Cronimet, a company based in Switzerland and a shareholder in MSA, a detail confirmed by Bensusan and Cronimet. Furthermore, investigators found that Cronimet shipped all of the ore to Thailand Smelting and Refining Company Ltd. (Thaisarco), the company frequently mentioned by UN investigators as a major processor of eastern Congo minerals.[26]

By any measure, the situation in eastern Congo is a finely interwoven mesh well beyond the control of the Congolese government or its military, both of which clearly seem unwilling to untangle the issues and deal with them one by one. How, then, can profiteers be expected to regulate the industry, stop conflicts, and alleviate the suffering of the citizenry? It is no wonder that private entrepreneurs are taking advantage of the confusion. The world wants and needs the rich minerals of eastern Congo, and leaving them buried in the ground is not an option. But do so many people have to die because of them? Who is at fault? What needs to be done? The answers are elusive. To find them, I must look far beyond the Congo.

15

RESOLUTION AND ILLUSION

I N MID-SEPTEMBER 2009, the tin-smelting company Thaisarco, owned by the British firm Amalgamated Metals Corporation (AMC), stopped buying tin ore from eastern Congo in a drastic move with repercussions throughout eastern Congo. Company officials did it grudgingly, blaming bad publicity about their Congolese operations. Giles Robbins, the chairman of Thaisarco and director of AMC, said the company's decision "has not been taken lightly," knowing that the move would likely make the region's artisanal miners and militias desperate enough to pursue extreme measures to sell their ore. Frustration oozed from the company's statement, since the firm had been quietly forging a procedure to identify and preclude the purchase of conflict minerals. Ironically, the first phase had gone into effect in July 2009, at the same time Global Witness released its scathing report.

Robbins chafed that AMC, among others, had been targeted, "despite significant progress towards implementation . . . of the [due diligence] initiative." He complained that advocacy groups continued to sabotage badly needed progress toward creating a workable procedure. "Negative campaigning from advocacy groups and adverse coverage in sections of the international media is undermining the credibility of the process. Although acting entirely lawfully, the threat of misleading and bad publicity remains for anyone who participates in the [eastern Congo] tin trade. These pressures have led Thaisarco to suspend its purchases from the [eastern Congo]. It is not alone in this respect as other European companies have already suspended their trading operations, although Thaisarco is the first smelter to do so."[1]

Robbins went on to say that "Thaisarco designed a certification scheme" known as the International Tin Research Institute's (ITRI) Tin Supply Chain Initiative (iTSCi) that provided for documentation of every bag of ore coming out of the region. Robbins called it "a practical and constructive approach to improving the visibility" of mines, minerals, and their masters in eastern Congo. More important, Robbins underscored that "it is the only viable scheme which has been developed by anyone in the tin industry, and the approach has been adopted as a benchmark for others servicing the mining sector."[2]

As the only concrete step taken by anyone, anywhere, to cut the connection between minerals mining and the humanitarian disaster taking place in eastern Congo, the Thaisarco plan was one to which all other nations and industries, including the global electronics industry and even the US Congress, would eventually have to turn. Once implemented, the plan could apply to all of the conflict minerals: gold and the so-called three Ts: tin, tantalum, and tungsten. Support for the process would come from many corners since it allowed everyone—*négociants, comptoirs,* foreign mineral buyers, smelters, component manufacturers, and electronics manufacturers—to claim they'd done their due diligence to block the use of conflict minerals in their businesses and products.

Among the iTSCi's supporters was an organization called the Global e-Sustainability Initiative (GeSI), a nebulous entity that described itself as a group of "leading [information and communications technology] companies—including telecommunications service providers and manufacturers as well as industry associations—and non-governmental organisations committed to achieving sustainability objectives through innovative technology."[3] Another was the Electronic Industry Citizenship Coalition (EICC), a group of international suppliers of raw materials and product manufacturers who had developed an industry code of conduct that "establishes standards to ensure that working conditions in the electronics industry supply chain are safe, that workers are treated with respect and dignity, and that business operations are environmentally responsible."[4] A third was the Tantalum-Niobium International Study Center (TIC).

Luis Neves, chairman of the GeSI, stated the obvious with sufficient gravity to make it sound original: "The implementation of a credible tracking scheme is necessary for the on-going exportation of conflict-free materials from the DRC. GeSI and the EICC are supportive of the iTSCi pilot as it is critical to the learnings [sic] and development of such a scheme."[5] So who were these people? Neves named names. "Downstream users of tin and tantalum in the electronics sector are making a substantial joint contribution of finance and/or products through EICC/GeSI (including companies such as Analog Devices, Apple, Cabot Supermetals, Dell, EMC Corporation, HP, IBM, Intel, Lenovo, Microsoft, Motorola Foundation, Nokia, Nokia Siemens Networks, Philips, RIM, Sony, Talison, Telefonica S.A., Western Digital and Xerox) in order to allow the project to work in conjunction with and support their own activities in the extractives sector."[6]

Even though a due diligence initiative had been formulated, a serious and sustained effort would be needed to solve the problem of conflict minerals in eastern Congo—not the headline-grabbing, name-and-shame tactics often employed by advocacy groups. AMC executive Robbins suggested in a press statement that "most experts on the Congo recognise that perfection in due diligence is not possible to achieve in the short term due to [the] enormity of the task—the minerals are produced by up to two million artisanal miners (according to the World Bank) operating in a country the size of Western Europe with a very limited infrastructure." Robbins appealed for support and assistance from advocacy groups to establish the minerals identification process. "We believe the mineral trade, working with key stakeholders could, given the constructive engagement of all advocacy groups, be the catalyst for the return of security and economic prosperity to the Congo."[7] Fighting the due diligence battle had been a Sisyphean task, Robbins complained, conceding that international pressure had affected business. "Customers are saying we don't want your tin if it is of [Congolese] origin," he told the *Times* in London. "What we need to resume trade is the clear and unequivocal support of the UN for the [proposed] regime."[8] But that was unlikely to come.

Harold Sher, chief executive of AMC, told the London *Times* that while no certification system is perfect, a flawed system was better than none and would allow European companies to resume mineral buying in eastern Congo. This was not simply bottom-line motivation, Sher explained. Asian buyers and processors could be much less concerned about human rights in eastern Congo and impervious to Western advocacy groups, yet they stood ready to fill the massive void created in the minerals market by the Thaisarco withdrawal from eastern Congo. About 20 to 30 percent of the Congo's tin and related ores were already being bought by Chinese and Indian companies largely divorced from certification procedures and disinterested in what happens in and around the mines. With some 70 percent of the Congo's tin ore suddenly available, the Chinese and Indian companies could easily capture the entire market. Sher predicted the end result: "The trade will deflect into less transparent hands."[9]

AMC's decision to stop buying ore from the Congo was not the first, of course. Four months earlier, in April 2009, the Belgium-based minerals merchant Traxys, which was linked by the UN experts to tin and coltan ore purchases from FDLR-controlled mines, had ceased buying there as well.

The cumulative effect was bad for local tin traders, who railed against the United Nations and advocacy groups for choking off vital income for hundreds of thousands of miners and their families and friends. Speaking for the mineral dealers of the region, John Kanyoni delineated growing desperation. "More than 70 percent of production from North and South Kivu was going to Thaisarco. It will be quite difficult for the sector to survive."[10]

The decision also blunted production at the Thaisarco smelting operation, which reportedly got a quarter to half of its tin ore from eastern Congo, according to an AMC spokesman. Since much of that Congolese tin ore came from the Bisie mine, Thaisarco and other smelters had to look elsewhere for supplies. But they didn't have to look far, since eastern Congo provides only 5 percent or less of the world's tin. The Thaisarco smelter is located in Phuket, Thailand, where about 260 people work in the plant. The smelter is one of the few industrial employers in the region and it was surprised to find itself in the midst of an international controversy. Michael Spratt, the managing director of the company, told a Thai journalist: "Thaisarco is an important value adder in the Phuket and the Thai economy. While our direct employment . . . is around 260 Thai people, I estimate that we create indirect employment throughout Thailand for about 1,500 others. In addition to [Thaisarco] being a highly responsible employer and significant tax payer, . . . Thailand consumes about 6,000 tons of tin a year and Thaisarco supplies most of it."[11]

Certification and Salvation

In June 2010, the global tin association ITRI provides me with details about the minerals due diligence certification system it has developed that is in the process of being implemented. The system is relatively simple and straightforward, but of course will be only as effective as the people who use it want it to be. To begin with, each mine in the region would be numbered, and copious detail about the mine would be documented during visits either by a representative of the ITRI or by a representative from a contracted nonprofit organization. Once "certified," the mine would be assigned identification tags. These tags would be given to government representatives from one of several agencies involved in monitoring mines and mining in eastern Congo. Among them is the Service d'Assistance et d'Encadrement des Small Scale Mines (SAESSCAM), a Congolese agency created to help artisanal miners. Another could be the Centre d'Evaluation, d'Expertise et de Certification (CEEC), an agency that focuses on certification.

Because almost all the mineral ore is loaded into plastic flour bags, each of the bags would be tagged once they are gathered in any locale, typically the small regional markets. The initial buyers—*négociants*— would fill out a report that details the number of bags, what is in them, and their mine of origin. When the collected minerals move on to the next stop, either a cooperative or a *comptoir*, all the relevant information would again be recorded and be consolidated into a *comptoir's* report. This information would accompany the ore as it travels across Africa, onto the ore ships, and then onward to smelters in South and Southeast Asia. It would then be available for all, including component and electronics manufacturers.

In mid-July 2010, Kay Nimmo, the manager of sustainability and regulatory affairs with ITRI, explains that two mines, Bisie in North Kivu and Nyabibwe in South Kivu, will be test locations for the new tagging system. ITRI has contracted with a local firm of geologists and engineers, BEGEM, to set up the project and run the pilot program. These geologists and engineers will explain it locally and hopefully elicit the necessary support. They will also give out and collect the tags and relevant data. Vehicles, cameras, and computers have been provided. The test runs will determine if the system is, in fact, practical, what data can be accurately collected, and what else might be needed to make the tracking a success. The test runs will reveal what means surface to circumvent the system. If it goes well, traceability will be expanded to more sites as funding becomes available.

Each tag has a unique number, name, and bar code. Trackers can theoretically use scanners to instantly record numbers and relevant data, but due to the lack of computer equipment and Internet access, the tag numbers will at first be recorded manually, along with records on bag contents and weight. This information will then be entered into an online database that can be used to track missing tag numbers or changes in bag weights as the minerals move through the system. Meanwhile, contract staff will be visiting the mines, meeting with miners and mine managers to convince them to support the tracking plan. These visits will begin the documentation of military and social conditions at each mine, hopefully leading to an accurate assessment.

The system seems about as workable as any, but some pitfalls are obvious. First and foremost is certification. This is crucial, since only ore from mines that are certified as conflict free can be ethically purchased.

While designation of mines as conflict or conflict-free is a desirable goal, providing an honest evaluation of each is highly problematic. Given the appropriately placed antagonism against the Hutu FDLR militia, any mines controlled by the Hutu FDLR would likely be banned as conflict mines, especially if those sympathetic to the government's position control the designation process. Likewise, any mines controlled by the former Tutsi militia, the CNDP, which has been incorporated into the Congolese army, and mines controlled by the Congolese army itself would presumably be designated conflict-free, even if the government forces are committing fraud, theft, and human rights abuses, which has often been the case.

The fairness of these designations, or the lack of it, affects the livelihoods of the miners perhaps more than the militias, however.

How much cajoling, bribery, and fakery is necessary to get the highly desired "conflict-free" designation for any given mine? What would it take for conflict-free status to be awarded to a mine that is not conflict-free? The militia could easily fade into the jungle for a few days when inspectors come to evaluate the mine. Local miners could then work freely, not under the gaze of hostile armed militia commanders. But couldn't such militias quickly move back into control once the inspectors and *négociants* are gone?

This messy problem is one that the ITRI decided early on to avoid. In an October 2009 document, the association said, "The tin industry is not in a position to make a decision on its own about which mines may be acceptable and which ones may be unacceptable. Such a decision has political as well as social ramifications and it is suggested that it would be best made by a coalition of interested parties (including the UN and the [Congolese] Government)."[12] While calling for a coalition of interested parties to designate the status of the mines, ITRI also suggested that the certifications be graded on various levels of freedom from conflict as a way to encourage mines and militias to move from conflict to conflict-free status.

One wonders how the Bisie mine, for example, might be designated. The Bisie mine is said to be the source of 70 percent of the region's tin ore, but it is also the nexus of fighting and mixed militia–Congolese army control. Would it be granted some sort of interim status? Considering the number of miners, military, and government officials involved in the Bisie mine, to say nothing of the *négociants*, *comptoirs*, and foreign mineral buyers, it seems more than likely it would be certified as conflict-free, regardless of the reality.

Beyond the designation, other potential problems are obvious. Given the remoteness of mines and the small local markets where raw ore is purchased from miners, what is to prevent tags from "good" mines from being put on ore bags from "bad" mines? The reality is that most ore is carried on the backs of miners to local markets. This is the case with the Bisie mine, which despite its size and production is virtually inaccessible except by footpath. *Négociants* will have little choice but to believe a miner who claims his ore comes from a conflict-free mine. And if the claim is denied, a small amount of cash or even the promise of a portion of future proceeds would undoubtedly be enough to get the right kind of tag put on any given bag of ore, no matter the mine of origin. Once tagged as "good" ore, that bag would be moved all the way to the smelter. The man with the tags, whether an independent person or a government agent, becomes the most important man at the mine on buying day.

However flawed it may be, the due diligence system will certainly solve a lot of problems for the mining industry. Since all ore bags will bear tags, and all of the ore purchases and shipments will be documented with detailed reports of origin, the entire system can be said to have been "cleaned up" regardless of the reality. The ore miners are now clean, the *négociants* are now clean, the *comptoirs* are now clean, the smelters are now clean, the component manufacturers, and ultimately the electronics companies and all others who use these metals, are clean too, by fiat. Due diligence has been done. The campaigners and activists can proclaim victory and report to their funders that their money has been well spent.

Congress Gets Involved

A wide-ranging due diligence certification process would be highly useful for the entire industry, especially since activist groups in the United States have recently spurred several members of the US Congress into the conflict minerals fray. In 2009, two bills were introduced, one in each house, to fix the problem of conflict minerals. The bills captured the attention of the electronics industry, which uses 60 percent of the world's coltan, and the United States is quite possibly the biggest consumer of these products. Rules and regulations that affect that market have to be taken seriously.

Senate Bill 891, titled the Congo Conflict Minerals Act of 2009, was jointly sponsored by senators often associated with African issues: Sam Brownback, an activist Republican from Kansas; Dick Durbin, a Democrat from Illinois; and Russ Feingold, a Wisconsin Democrat. The verbiage surrounding the bill was passionate and determined but requires some scrutiny. "Metals derived from inhumanely mined minerals go into electronic products used by millions of Americans," Brownback said of the bill, without mentioning how much or where the metals originate. Do inhumane mining conditions include those of major producers in China, Indonesia, Bolivia, and Peru?

He went on: "In the Democratic Republic of Congo, many people—especially women and children—are victimized by armed groups who are trying to make a profit from mining 'conflict minerals.'" Very true, of course, but these armed groups include the Congolese army and the ex-Tutsi CNDP militia, which has become part of the Congolese army. Shouldn't the senator have been talking about this to the Congolese government?

"The legislation introduced today brings accountability and transparency to the supply chain of minerals used in the manufacturing of many electronic devices," Brownback continued. "I hope the legislation will help save lives."[13] For that accountability and transparency to be credible, accurate records from far beyond the borders of the United States and regions well beyond the reach of the US Congress would be required.

Co-sponsor Durbin added: "Without knowing it, tens of millions of people in the United States may be putting money in the pockets of some of the worst human rights violators in the world, simply by using a cell phone or laptop computer. We ought to do all we can to make sure that the products we use and the minerals we import, in no way support those who violate human rights abroad."[14] Since the vast majority of these minerals come from China, Indonesia, Bolivia, and Peru, Durbin seemed to suggest that these countries have horrendous human rights records. He could be right.

Much of the passion over conflict minerals has emerged from the rape epidemic in eastern Congo (detailed in chapter 5), a tool of war designed to humiliate and destroy families and communities. But one has to wonder at the logic behind the advocacy groups' desire to choke off the supply of money to the "armed groups" responsible for the rape epidemic. The rape problem permeates society. The "armed groups" include the Congolese police, the Congolese army, the former Tutsi CNDP militia, *and* the Hutu FDLR. Will shutting off the flow of money into the region stop rape? It could have the opposite effect. Miners, along with their families and friends, will likely be more victimized, not less victimized, if soldiers and their commanders—army or militia—are dirt poor and desperate for food, money, and whatever they can get at the point of a gun.

In language typical of congressional mandates relating to Africa, the bill proclaimed that the United States would *support* efforts to investigate, monitor, and stop activities involving "natural resources that contribute to illegally armed groups and human rights violations in eastern Congo." The key requirement in the bill was that US companies selling products that contain coltan, tin, or tungsten must disclose to the Securities and Exchange Commission the origin of these metals and minerals. Such a due diligence process was well underway under the ITRI scheme. However, nearly eighteen months after the Senate bill was introduced, it was still languishing in committee.

In the House, meanwhile, a similar bill, H.R. 4128, titled the Conflict Minerals Trade Act, was sponsored by Representative Jim McDermott, a Democrat from Washington State. The bill proposed a procedure for importers of foreign goods to identify their products as conflict mineral free, or not, much as food producers are required to label the contents and calories inside their packages. It's hard to imagine, however, that a company with a profit motive would put a label on its product that reads: Warning—This Product Contains Conflict Minerals.

McDermott announced the bill while surrounded by a cadre of advocates from the World Vision aid organization, the Enough Project, Global Witness, and the trade group known as the Information Technology Industry Council. Beating the drum of activism, McDermott dove into a pool of inspirational rhetoric that typifies the emotions that conflict minerals have sparked. "Under my legislation, the American people, and the world, will know when a company or industry is using conflict minerals and I think this knowledge will prove much more powerful than any weapon fired by those prosecuting this horrible war. This bill can fire a shot that will be heard round the world."[15] In late April 2010, when the bill was approved by the House Foreign Affairs Committee, McDermott said enthusiastically, "This bill will empower companies and consumers to know which products—including things like cell phones, laptops, and other goods—are made with or without minerals that have helped fund the brutal conflict in the DRC."[16]

Ultimately, both bills were condensed into a minor provision of the massive financial reform bill approved by Congress in July 2010, one of the milestones of the Obama administration. The provision requires that any company that uses tin, tungsten, tantalum, or gold in its products must disclose the origin of the minerals to the Securities and Exchange Commission, especially if they come from the Congo, Rwanda, Uganda, or Burundi. Audits must verify the reports. The bill drew opposition from industry, especially the country's jewelers, who make their livings selling gold. As detailed in previous chapters, UN experts have tracked the large volume of gold that flows from mines in eastern Congo through Uganda, Rwanda, Burundi, and Tanzania to major markets in Dubai. And from there, who knows where? Tracing, tracking, and verifying the sources will be nothing short of a nightmare. It will be interesting to see those reports when and if they are ever produced.

Even before the conflict minerals provision became law, the campaigners had found a friend in the Obama administration. Robert Hormats, the undersecretary of state for economic, energy, and agricultural affairs, is the most outspoken of government officials when it comes to conflict minerals. He takes on the cause of improving the situation in eastern Congo with missionary zeal. Hormats has a grounded understanding of the issue and admits that fixing the problem goes well beyond passing a bill in Congress, launching name-and-shame campaigns, or convening people to sit in European boardrooms to set guidelines and procedures for bags of ore mined in jungle enclaves on distant continents. "First, we must accept a simple, but uncompromising truth: there are no quick fixes. Lasting solutions require long term investments of time, energy, and resources," Hormats said in a May 2010 address. "Second, we must note that the challenge posed by illegal or unregulated extraction of natural resources touches upon a wide range of issues: human rights, economic stability, good governance, development, trade, state authority, and national security. Therefore, our response must be equally extensive."[17]

As the US Congress took a step toward addressing the conflict minerals problem, the United Nations began its worrisome withdrawal from the Congo. A unit of about one hundred Senegalese soldiers went home just before June 30, 2010, the fiftieth anniversary of Congo's independence. "I think we . . . recognize [the UN mission] has been here 10 years and we have to evolve and adapt," said Alan Doss, the departing head of the UN force first sent into the Congo by the UN in 2000. Doss admitted that even though the Congolese government said the UN was no longer needed or wanted, progress in the country had been marginal. "We can push out an armed group, but if the state doesn't come in with police, justice, roads, schools, then it won't make a big difference."[18] As part of the withdrawal, the name of the UN program would be changed from the French acronym MONUC to MONUSCO, part of a mission change from peacekeeping to civilian protection. Doss was replaced by Roger Meece, former US ambassador to Kinshasa. The total drawdown of forces was said to be only about two thousand initially, with future withdrawals to be determined, leaving the people of eastern Congo, as always, facing an unknown fate.

Update: Lessons Learned

In late 2010, the international tin association, ITRI, released the results of its three-month pilot program to test its "bag and tag" system of tracking minerals flowing out of the eastern Congo. The association's mine tags were distributed by government mine agents for about three hundred tons of tin ore coming out of the South Kivu province. (The area is still largely controlled by the Hutu FDLR militia, but it is increasingly being taken over by Congolese forces.) As expected, the lack of adequate technological support prevented the tags' bar codes from being scanned electronically; the data for each bag was recorded by hand. The *négociants* purchased the bags, and if they either consolidated or "upgraded" the ore by removing some of the impurities, it was retagged. The ore bags, often with two tags, were then purchased by the *comptoirs*, and the relevant information was fed into a central database, showing that minerals could be traced from miner to exporter.

The system was found to work for the most part, but there were problems, of course, many along the lines of what I and others had feared. According to the association's report, *Technical Challenges Encountered & Solutions Developed in the iTSCi Pilot Project in South Kivu*, the system was subject to fraud and abuse. For example, the mines operated around the clock in some cases, but the government agents responsible for tagging bags of ore worked only during the day. In addition, the government did not provide enough agents to carry out the system, and the agents were poorly and infrequently paid, which caused agents to use their positions to their personal advantage. In some cases, agents reportedly demanded payments of five dollars per tag. There also remained the widespread informal and illegal collection of taxes on miners and buyers, including taxes or "safe passage" fees charged by the militias and the Congolese army, which was present at most mine sites; these practices cannot be fixed by the tracking system itself, the association noted.[19]

Since the bags were weighed as they moved through the system, it was found that they gained an average of twenty pounds from the miner to the *comptoir*. This suggests that ore from so-called conflict mines may have been added along the way. (Other explanations were possible, however, such as bags breaking and spilling then being refilled.) There were other problems: tags were lost during the process; logbooks were ruined by rain, wear, and tear; some traders tried to reuse tags; tags were stolen; logbook data was incorrect and/or illegible.

Of the eight thousand tags issued by the association, about three-quarters of them ended up in the hands of the *comptoirs*, which indicates a roughly 75 percent success rate for the system. But with the pilot project completed, the association struggled to expand the system so that it would work throughout the region. That is a costly proposition, one that few in either the mining industry or the electronics industry are willing to fund. As of this writing, moving to the second, expanded phase of the tracking system has been suspended until an international agreement can be found to support it financially and administratively.

Looming, however, are strict reporting requirements for anyone in the United States who produces products, ranging from electronics to jewelry, that may include minerals from the eastern Congo. These rules, in effect as of April 2011, are being imposed as a result of the sweeping financial reform act discussed in the previous section. They require a company to certify that no metals in any of its products come from conflict mines. Without a tracking system in place, however, industry officials rightly worry that the new rules will promptly shut down the mining industry in the eastern Congo. Since such a small percentage of the global supply of metals comes from the region, these mines are simply not worth the time, trouble, and cost, not to mention the negative publicity.

The end result, sadly, will be that miners of the eastern Congo, who some say number about two million, will be left without incomes. Those who wish to continue will be forced to find other, possibly illegal channels to sell their ore, giving rise once again to armed groups, be they militias or the Congolese military, that can control the clandestine export of minerals. As Western companies cease doing business in the region, that void most certainly will be filled by businesses not bound by the conflict-free mineral mandate, quite possibly Chinese and/or Southeast Asian enterprises unconcerned about the stigma of human rights abuses. Those unwilling or unable to participate in continued mining will be more desperate than ever, resulting in renewed violence, recreating the conditions in eastern Congo that human rights campaigners have tried to eliminate.

EPILOGUE

THE HORROR AND
THE HOPE

JOSEPH CONRAD'S novella *Heart of Darkness* was published in 1902 and was drawn from his six-month voyage up the Congo River in 1890. At the time, the country was known as the Congo Free State, a vast expanse of jungle and mountains the size of Europe and claimed as private property by Belgium's King Leopold. Conrad's fictional narrator describes a trip up the Congo in search of the notorious Mr. Kurtz, whose fevered death he attends. Kurtz's final words are: "The horror! The horror!"

Conrad's work set the theme, tone, and even characters for almost all of the literary and journalistic work about the Congo that has followed. The story that Conrad told about the Congo has not changed much in over a century. It continues to be a land of chaos, carnage, and plunder.

The argument has been made that the chaos derives from precedents set by Europeans in their exploitation. As exemplified by the amoral company man Kurtz, Europeans brought a previously unknown brand of inhumane behavior that seared the soul of a continent.

I witnessed something of this while researching *First Kill Your Family: Child Soldiers of Uganda and the Lord's Resistance Army.*

These rebels in Uganda routinely butchered their fellow tribesmen with machetes, smashed their heads, and cut off lips, noses, ears, and women's breasts, even forcing stunned survivors to eat the dead. These were savage acts, perhaps spurred by some pathological impulse to see other humans suffer excruciating pain. Some suggest that the Ugandan rebels' behavior echoed what the Europeans did a hundred years ago in the Congo, which left an estimated ten million Congolese dead.

Why has such savagery persisted? Who's at fault? Can Africa and the Congolese rise above the past?

The malaise in eastern Congo is an ongoing humanitarian disaster. One needs to experience it to understand it. No one can come away untouched or unchanged. I continue to be perplexed at how so much death in the Congo could have occurred and continued so long yet gone virtually unnoticed in the outside world.

Progress seems to be just around the bend. But even so, miners may resist change because they don't want to lose their income, even if it means sharing their profits with armed groups. The middlemen may be more than happy to apply a "don't ask, don't tell" rule to mineral purchases, also fearful of their livelihood. Now foreign companies are instituting tracking procedures for conflict minerals so that everyone can keep working. No one wants to be cut out of the process.

The irony is that many digging in the mines in eastern Congo carry the same mobile phones and crave the same laptop computers said to be the cause of war and death in their region. They all want to benefit from the technology they have helped create with the minerals they dig, even though many have suffered tragically.

What can and should be done to solve the problems in eastern Congo?

Recent attention has focused on the foreign companies that buy the minerals in the Congo and the electronics manufacturers who use these metals in their products. These companies are the source of the money flowing into the Congo, passing from the company representatives and mineral buyers into the hands of *comptoirs*, *négociants*, and ultimately to the militias and miners. Some of it goes to governmental fees and taxes and undoubtedly into the pockets of officials.

Foreign companies operating in the Congo are easy targets for activists. International corporations writhe under the harsh lights of such publicity. It seems more effective to go after them than to criticize the Congolese government, which is ultimately responsible for eastern Congo.

Global corporations, however, have responded by developing a due diligence process that is slowly being implemented. While it may not be foolproof, it is an attempt to stop the flow of conflict minerals into global markets. The groundswell of support for the due diligence process, of course, comes from the fact that companies up and down the mineral supply chain can use it to deflect the accusations that they and electronics consumers have been funding the worst human death toll since World War II.

Advocacy groups admittedly have made monumental strides in raising public awareness of the problems in eastern Congo. That success rides on the premise that most popular electronic devices contain significant amounts of high-tech metals with their bloody origins in eastern Congo. Unfortunately, this premise is very misleading. A case in point is a spoof on the PC-versus-Mac television advertisement by Apple posted on the Enough Project website. In it, a man representing a PC pulls rocks from his pocket, saying they are tin, tantalum, and tungsten. He then says, "A lot of this stuff comes from the Congo," and goes on to say that hundreds of million of dollars in profits are being made.

Less than 5 percent of the world's supply of tin comes from the Congo, and only about 10 percent of the world's tantalum comes from eastern Congo and its neighbors. Even some tungsten originates there. Yet activists have avoided discussing the actual amount of these minerals originating in the Congo and entering the global markets, leaving the impression that all of our electronics are loaded with Congolese metals and are therefore dripping with blood.

While the amount of minerals may be small, it does not diminish the problem in eastern Congo or its decade of death. Rather, it enlarges the question: how could so many die as a result of the mining there? The answer points to other, deeper issues such as ethnic animosities that have been present for much longer than the recent mining activities. Increasingly, one must consider that mining profits may only have exacerbated a longstanding problem, not created it. Curtailing or eliminating the mining probably won't make the problem go away.

Are the producers and consumers of electronics really at fault in eastern Congo? If corporate blame is to be dispensed, it needs to be directed to all, including the aerospace industry and the medical profession, even nuclear power. One of the popular uses of tungsten is for fly fishing hooks. Are fly fishermen to blame for the violence in eastern Congo?

In fact, we're all to blame. We all use and depend on all sorts of high-tech devices in our daily lives. The cellular phones and computers we use clearly connect us with people in many corners of the world. So do the jet engines that carry us around the world. So do the medical implants we use to improve our health. So do the digital cameras we use and the eyeglasses we wear. So does nuclear power, each and every time we flick on a light switch. We are all linked on our shrinking planet. This is why the work by advocacy groups fighting to stop the purchase of conflict minerals is valuable. They have forced a disinterested world to become aware of itself and others.

I am reminded of a meditative essay written by the Vietnamese Zen Buddhist master Thich Nhat Hanh. In it, he takes the reader through the exercise of considering what goes into the existence of a daisy. There must be the fertile soil, the rain, the seeds, the air, the sunshine, and the shade. The same sun that shines on the daisy touches all corners of the planet. Rain is the result of clouds that form out of moisture that comes from distant lands and seas. The fertile soil comes from season after season when other plants have lived, died, and decomposed. In this meditation, one can open worlds far beyond the five senses. One can recognize "inter-being," that no man is an island, that each of us is connected in many ways to everything else on the planet. The realization can be humbling. It makes one pause in the pursuit of personal ends to ask if we are mindlessly ignoring the world, or are we mindful that our daily actions and decisions connect us with the rest of the planet?

Cellular phones and computers connect us all in many ways. Ore from Asia, Southeast Asia, South America, Australia, and even the eastern Congo is mined and shipped to smelters in Russia, India, and Southeast Asia. From there, the metals are distributed to component makers in still other locations. These parts are then assembled into our phones and laptops. When we cradle a phone to our ear and when we place our laptop on the table of our neighborhood coffee shop, not only is the world at our fingertips and within the sound of our voice, but it is also literally in our hands.

Where to Go from Here

This brings us back to eastern Congo. Name-and-shame campaigns may draw attention to the malaise in eastern Congo, and such campaigns certainly have prompted due diligence procedures that hopefully will end the purchase of minerals from the Congo's conflict mines.

But real solutions for the eastern Congo cannot be imposed from outside. The Congolese must create their own solutions to their problems. The key to solving the conflict minerals puzzle lies within the people of eastern Congo and their government. It will take the application of truth and integrity for the due diligence process to work, for example. Can the estimated two million people in eastern Congo who are involved in minerals and mining rise to the task? Can the local, regional, and national leaders forgo the temptation to enrich themselves at the expense of their fellow countrymen? Will the people of the Congo demand to have the kind of leadership and government they so badly need and deserve?

Rather than engaging in aggressive public relations tactics, rights campaigners, advocacy groups, and others might better become involved in eastern Congo in more meaningful ways. Activists have choices. They can sit in air-conditioned offices in high-rise buildings in urban centers around the world, using their cellular phones and computers to complain about global corporations and the global economy while conducting studies and making passionate pronouncements.

Or they can sit in mud huts, face to face with the beleaguered miners and the rape victims that populate the villages in eastern Congo. They can work on the ground, day after day, hand in hand with the growing cadre of Congolese who struggle to bring their country out of the ashes of war and destruction. They can meet with local officials and urge them to do the right thing.

Forming personal and long-lasting bonds with people is the most effective and powerful way to effect change. The world shifts one person at a time, one mind at a time. People need to know you before they can trust you, believe you, or respond to you. Flying in from distant cities, scuffing the dirt, and sniffing the air for a few weeks is not enough. Feet on the ground followed by time, toughness, and commitment to change is needed. Nothing less.

ACKNOWLEDGMENTS

I WANT to thank Congolese journalist Jacques Kahorha of Goma, who provided invaluable assistance and support during my extended stays in eastern Democratic Republic of the Congo. Besides being an excellent journalist, he is one of the shining lights of eastern Congo, who keeps afloat all within his vast circle of family, friends, and acquaintances. In Sudan, I must thank Ahmed el-Sheikh of Khartoum, whose undying enthusiasm and talent as a journalist ignited an otherwise bleak landscape. At the Institute for War & Peace Reporting, I want to thank director Tony Borden for his vision of a world in which journalists from all lands can have their voices heard. At Chicago Review Press, I want to thank editor Sue Betz, who shares an expansive vision of the world and works hard to ensure that anyone who cares can read about it. I also thank my agent, Michele Rubin, who opened doors that once seemed forever closed. Finally, I want to thank my wife, Dina, whose unwavering confidence and support has made it possible to weather storms on landscapes familiar and foreign.

NOTES

---

1. The Mandro Hut

1. The child soldiers who formed the basis of Kony's army are the subject of my book *First Kill Your Family: Child Soldiers of Uganda and the Lord's Resistance Army* (Chicago: Lawrence Hill Books, 2009).

2. Village of the Skulls

1. International Criminal Court, *Situation in the Democratic Republic of the Congo: Germain Katanga and Mathieu Ngudjolo Chui* (combined factsheet, June 27, 2008), 10.
2. Ibid., 11.
3. Ibid., 12.
4. Ibid., 12.
5. Ibid., 12.
6. Ibid., 11.

3. Gold from Blood

1. AngloGold Ashanti, *Country Report DRC 07*, www.anglogoldashanti.com /NR/rdonlyres/0F71E463-1ABA-4A34-AF45-565E1DBD996A/0/drc.pdf, 4.
2. Ibid., 5.
3. Ibid., 14.
4. Ibid., 10.
5. Ibid., 14.
6. Human Rights Watch, *The Curse of Gold* (New York: Human Rights Watch, 2005), 18.

7. United Nations Security Council, *Report of the Panel of Experts on the Illegal Exploitation of Natural Resources and Other Forms of Wealth of the Democratic Republic of the Congo* (United Nations Security Council document S/2001/357, April 12, 2001), 12.

8. Human Rights Watch, *The Curse of Gold*, 22.

9. Ibid., 25.

10. Ibid., 21.

11. Ibid., 26.

12. Ibid., 27.

13. Ibid., 28.

14. Ibid., 29.

15. Ibid., 32.

16. Ibid., 33.

17. Ibid., 35.

18. Ibid., 36.

19. Ibid., 37.

20. Ibid., 39.

21. Ibid., 41.

22. Ibid., 42.

6. The Agony of Abyei

1. See *First Kill Your Family: Child Soldiers of Uganda and the Lord's Resistance Army* (Chicago: Lawrence Hill Books, 2009), 183–242.

2. *Sudan Tribune*, "Sudan Arrests Kidnappers of Chinese Oil Workers—Minister," December 18, 2008, www.sudantribune.com/spip .php?article29623.

7. A Tale of Two Sudans

1. Missy Ryan, "Iraq Civilian Death Toll Down to 4,500 in 09: Study," Reuters, January 1, 2010.

2. Mahmood Mamdani, *Saviors and Survivors: Darfur, Politics, and the War on Terror* (New York: Pantheon Books, 2009), 52.

3. Ibid., 51.

4. Alaa Shahine, "Sudan Signs North Darfur Oil Exploration Agreement," Bloomberg News, February 2, 2010.

5. Ibid.

8. Armies and Exploitation

1. Dinesh Mahtani, Raymond Debelle, Mouctar Kokouma Diallo, Christian B. Dietrich, and Claudio Gramizzi, *Final Report of the Group of Experts on*

the Democratic Republic of the Congo (United Nations Security Council document S/2009/603, November 23, 2009), 7.

2. Dinesh Mahtani, Raymond Debelle, Mouctar Kokouma Diallo, Christian B. Dietrich, and Claudio Gramizzi, *Interim Report of the Group of Experts on the Democratic Republic of the Congo* (United Nations Security Council document S/2009/253, May 14, 2009), 6.

3. Ibid., 9.

4. Ibid., 9.

5. Ibid., 9–10.

6. Ibid., 10.

7. Ibid., 11–12.

8. Ibid., 12.

9. Ibid., 14.

10. Ibid., 13.

11. Ibid., 12.

12. Ibid., 21–22.

13. Ibid., 22.

14. Ibid., 22.

15. "About Us," Traxys official website, www.traxys.com/Gui/Content. aspx?Page=AboutUs.

16. "Trademet SA," Minor Metals Trade Association official website, www .mmta.co.uk/members/memberDetails.php?id=89.

17. Mahtani et al., *Interim Report*, 22.

18. Ibid., 22.

19. Franz Wild, "Traxys Says It Halts Buying of Tin from Congo from June 1," *Bloomberg News*, May 4, 2009.

20. Mahtani et al., *Interim Report*, 23.

21. Global Witness, "Summary," in *Faced with a Gun, What Can You Do?: War and the Militarisation of Mining in Eastern Congo* (London: Global Witness, July 2009), 4.

22. Ibid., 6.

11. Into Coltan Country

1. "Tantalum Overview," Grandview Materials official website, www .grandviewmaterials.com/tantalum.html.

2. Tantalum-Niobium International Study Center, e-mail message to author, June 19, 2010.

3. Ibid.

4. See ITRI official website, www.itri.co.uk.

5. ITRI, e-mail message to author, June 8, 2010.

14. Things Fall Apart

1. Global Witness, "DR Congo: Ex-rebels Take Over Mineral Trade Extortion Racket," news release, March 2010, www.globalwitness.org/library/dr-congo-ex-rebels-take-over-mineral-trade-extortion-racket.
2. Ibid.
3. Ibid.
4. Ibid.
5. Ibid.
6. BBC, "Germany Arrests Top Rwanda Rebels," November 17, 2009, http://news.bbc.co.uk/2/hi/8364507.stm.
7. Dinesh Mahtani, Raymond Debelle, Mouctar Kokouma Diallo, Christian B. Dietrich, and Claudio Gramizzi, *Final Report of the Group of Experts on the Democratic Republic of the Congo* (United Nations Security Council document S/2009/603, November 23, 2009), 24.
8. Ibid., 25.
9. Ibid., 25.
10. Max Delany and Scott Baldauf, "Germany Arrests Congo Rebel Leaders," *Christian Science Monitor*, November 17, 2009.
11. Ibid.
12. Ibid.
13. Mahtani et al., *Final Report*, 3.
14. Ibid., 8.
15. Ibid., 9.
16. Ibid., 17.
17. Ibid., 33.
18. Ibid., 34.
19. Ibid., 36.
20. Ibid., 38.
21. Ibid., 42.
22. Ibid., 44.
23. Published as "Annex 79," in Mahtani et al., *Final Report*, 209–210.
24. Published as "Annex 84" and "Annex 85" in Mahtani et al., *Final Report*, 216–217.
25. Mahtani et al., *Final Report*, 49.
26. Ibid., 51–52.

15. Resolution and Illusion

1. Giles Robbins, "Thaisarco Suspends Tin Ore Purchases from the Congo," news release, Amalgamated Metal Corporation, September 18, 2009.
2. Ibid.

3. Global e-Sustainability Initiative, "GeSI & EICC Join with Tantalum and Tin Supply Chain Representatives and Stakeholders on Responsible Sourcing of Minerals from Conflict Regions," news release, December 7, 2010, www.gesi.org/Media/PressReleaseFullstory/tabid/104/smid/503/ArticleID/69/reftab/61/Default.aspx.

4. "EICC Code of Conduct," Electronic Industry Citizenship Coalition official website, www.eicc.info/PDF/EICC%20Code%20of%20Conduct%20English.pdf.

5. ITRI, "DRC Ministry of Mines Reconfirms Official Support," news release, June 11, 2010, www.itri.co.uk/pooled/articles/BF_NEWSART/view.asp?Q=BF_NEWSART_319685.

6. ITRI, "Supply Chains Unite to Start iTSCi Mineral Traceability Project in DRC," news release, March 19, 2010, www.itri.co.uk/pooled/articles/BF_NEWSART/view.asp?Q=BF_NEWSART_318425.

7. Joe Bavier, "Thaisarco Suspends Congo Tin Ore Purchases," Reuters, September 18, 2009.

8. Carl Mortished, "AMC Threatens to Quit Congo in Row Over 'Rebel Links,'" Times (London), September 29, 2009, http://business.timesonline.co.uk/tol/business/industry_sectors/natural_resources/article6853057.ece.

9. Ibid.

10. Bavier, "Thaisarco Suspends Congo Tin Ore Purchases."

11. Alasdair Forbes, "Phuket Tin Smelter at Centre of International Row," Phuket Observer, July 23, 2009, www.phuketobserver.com/phuket-tin-smelter-at-centre-of-international-row/.

12. ITRI, ITRI Tin Supply Chain Initiative, version 2 (discussion paper, October 2009), www.itri.co.uk/SITE/UPLOAD/Document/iTSCi_Final_Version_2_English__2.10.09.pdf, 14.

13. Office of US Senator Sam Brownback, "Brownback, Durbin, Feingold Introduce Congo Conflict Minerals Act," news release, April 24, 2009, http://brownback.senate.gov/public/press/record.cfm?id=311956.

14. Ibid.

15. Office of US Representative Jim McDermott, "Rep. McDermott Introduces Conflict Minerals Trade Act," news release, November 19, 2009, http://mcdermott.house.gov/index.php?option=com_content&view=article&id=37.

16. Office of US Representative Jim McDermott, "Rep. McDermott's Conflict Minerals Bill Moves Forward After Foreign Affairs Committee Markup," news release, April 28, 2010, http://mcdermott.house.gov/index.php?option=com_content&view=article&id=325.

17. Robert D. Hormats, "Our Global Challenges: Improving the Resources Trade" (remarks to the CSIS–University of Miami Council on Foreign Relations Roundtable, Washington, DC, May 18, 2010).

18. Katrina Manson, "UN Peacekeepers Start Congo Withdrawal," Reuters, June 17, 2010.

19. ITRI, *Technical Challenges Encountered & Solutions Developed in the iTSCi Pilot Project in South Kivu* (2010), www.itri.co.uk/SITE/UPLOAD/Document/Problems_Solutions_and_Lessons_-_iTSCi_Pilot_-_English_-_final_text_comp_pics.pdf.

INDEX